THE ROAD FROM HOME

I began to hear whisperings—at home and at Grandma's, especially at night, when my parents thought we were asleep. But more than their whisperings, it was the way they looked, the way they talked and moved about, that made me know something was wrong. I began to hear words like "deportations," "massacres," "annihilation." I didn't like the sounds of the words, but mostly I didn't like the looks on their faces when they said these words.

The Road from Home

◀ THE STORY OF AN ARMENIAN GIRL ▶

By David Kherdian

A Beech Tree Paperback Book

NEW YORK

The Library of Congress has cataloged the Greenwillow Books
edition of *The Road from Home* as follows:
Kherdian, David. The road from home. Summary: A biography of
the author's mother concentrating on her childhood in Turkey before
the Turkish government deported its Armenian population.
ISBN 0-688-80205-2   ISBN 0-688-84205-4 lib. bdg.
1. Kherdian, Veron—Juvenile literature. 2. Armenians
in Turkey—Biography—Juvenile literature. 3. Children in
Turkey—Juvenile literature. 4. Armenian massacres, 1915-1923—
Juvenile literature. [1. Kherdian, Veron. 2. Armenians in Turkey—
Biography. 3. Armenian massacres, 1915-1923.] I. Title.
DR435.A7K47 949.6'1'01 [92] 78-72511

10
First Beech Tree Edition, 1995
ISBN 0-688-14425-X

To the Memory of Lousapere Dumehjian

September 16, 1916.—To the Government of Aleppo.

It was at first communicated to you that the government, by order of the Jemiet, had decided to destroy completely all the Armenians living in Turkey. . . . An end must be put to their existence, however criminal the measures taken may be, and no regard must be paid to either age or sex nor to conscientious scruples.

Minister of the Interior **TALAAT PASHA**

August 22, 1939.—I have given orders to my Death Units to exterminate without mercy or pity men, women, and children belonging to the Polish-speaking race. It is only in this manner that we can acquire the vital territory which we need. After all, who remembers today the extermination of the Armenians?

ADOLF HITLER

By the middle of the nineteenth century the once-powerful Ottoman Empire was in rapid dissolution. Territories had been lost from its lands in Africa, the Balkans and the Mediterranean, and the major European powers were beginning to vie with one another for the lion's share from the estate of what one statesman was to call the "Sick Man of Europe." The stage was being set for a revolutionary party, and in 1908 the party of Young Turks came to power, heralding the wobbly rise of modern Turkey and the eventual persecution of all its Christian minorities, in particular the Armenians.

The Young Turks began by forcing the "Red" Sultan Abdul Hamid (who had been responsible for the Armenian massacres of 1895-96) to accept a constitution founded on principles of liberty, equality, justice and fraternity.

A seemingly auspicious era commenced for the Armenians. Their political parties were allowed to function freely for the first time. Although they were allowed to sing previously prohibited folk and national songs, as well as patriotic songs that hailed the independence of an imagined Armenian state, the fate of the overwhelming majority of Armenians within the Ottoman Empire did not improve after the downfall of the "Red" Sultan.

At the same time, the Armenian revolutionary parties were ensuring their downfall by cooperating with the Turks, who, through their feigned complicity, were learning the secrets of the parties, while waiting for the opportune moment to realize their ultimate goal of accomplishing "Turkey for the Turks."

One year after the constitution, Sultan Abdul Hamid was dethroned and replaced by the elderly Sultan Muhammad V. A dictatorial government was established, with the sultan acting merely as a figurehead.

In April 1909, the Ittihat party (Union and Progress party), as the Young Turks came to be known, participated in a massacre in Adana and other Cilician districts. Thirty thousand Armenians were put to death, the majority of them being killed by a military contingent dispatched from Istanbul, presumably for the purpose of establishing order. This was perhaps the turning point for the Armenians, because instead of resisting, their revolutionary leaders and the Armenian members of Parliament tightened their bonds of friendship with the Turkish leaders, believing that this would be in the best interests of the Armenian nation.

The Ittihat party was no better than Sultan Abdul Hamid in stemming the dismemberment of the Ottoman Empire. Austria had annexed Bosnia and Herzegovina, Crete had declared union with Greece, and Bulgaria had won full independence before Abdul Hamid was deposed; Italy occupied Tripoli, and in 1912 Turkey was severely beaten in the Balkan War. It was able to retain only a small portion of its Balkan holdings, and the major portion of European Turkey had been lost.

Encouraged, the Armenians set up a delegation in 1912 in an effort to enlist the support of the European powers in establishing reforms with Turkish consent. The appointments that were made only further antagonized the Young Turks, despite the fact that nothing had been accomplished by the time World War I broke out.

On July 28, 1914, Austria declared war against the Serbs, and World War I formally commenced. On November 2, 1914, Russia and Serbia declared war on Turkey, an ally of Germany, followed by England and France on November 5.

Turkey was now ready to settle the "Armenian Question" once and for all. For this purpose, the Ittihat Central Committee convened in a secret meeting toward the beginning of 1915, deciding to exterminate every Armenian living on Turkish soil.

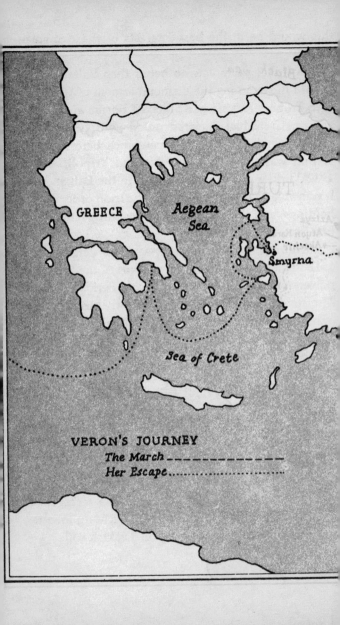

GREECE

Aegean
Sea

Smyrna

Sea of Crete

VERON'S JOURNEY
The March _ _ _ _ _ _ _ _ _ _
Her Escape..................

For as long as I knew the sky and the clouds, we lived in our white stucco house in the Armenian quarter of Aziza, in Turkey, but when the great dome of Heaven cracked and shattered over ourselves, and we were abandoned by the sun and slowly scattered seed across the Arabian desert... somewhere else and my Aziza, my precious somewhere was made to crumble and fall and forever disappearing as life

My father had gone to Afyon Karahisar to get his bride, and my grandmother used to say, When he brought out harss [bride] from Afyon, we had music and dancing for one week, and I made thirty-five trays of paklava [pastry] and thirty trays of kurabia [sugar cookies] for the wedding.

My grandmother's friends—Turkish, Greek and Armenian—all said, "Where did you find this girl? She looks like a country girl, tall and strong, and with such red cheeks."

◀ ONE ▶
1907–1913

For as long as I knew the sky and the clouds, we lived in our white stucco house in the Armenian quarter of Azizya, in Turkey, but when the great dome of Heaven cracked and shattered over our lives, and we were abandoned by the sun and blown like scattered seed across the Arabian desert, none returned but me, and my Azizya, my precious home, was made to crumble and fall and forever disappear from my life.

My father had gone to Afyon Karahissar to get his bride, and my grandmother used to say, "When he brought our *harss* [bride] from Afyon, we had music and dancing for one week, and I made thirty-five trays of *pahklava* [pastry] and thirty trays of *khourabia* [sugar cookies] for the wedding."

My grandmother's friends—Turkish, Greek and Armenian—all said, "Where did you find this girl? She looks like a country girl, tall and strong, and with such red cheeks."

My mother was gifted with her fingers, and she was strong and healthy. She was an expert weaver in addition to tending to her housework and her garden of vegetables and flowers.

I remember how she used to make *khashkash* from the poppy seeds. She would first brown the seeds in a frying pan and then grind them on a special stone. It made a kind of poppy-seed butter, and it was one of our staples. Every time she made a fresh batch she would invite her lady friends over for lunch. My mother was very gay and friendly, and she was always having her friends over because Father was away so much of the time on business.

Everyone in the family was especially fond of my mother, because my aunt, the other bride in my grandmother's home, was delicate and frail and unable to do hard work. She was sick most of the time, and they used to say, "*Vakh, vakh,* our boy's life has been burnt; this bride has come to nothing."

At that time, and in that region, a sick bride was considered the worst thing of all. We all lived under one roof then, with my grandparents and aunts and uncles, but when I was five, we moved, with my sick aunt and uncle and cousin, to the new Armenian quarter. There we had the acreage we needed for growing poppies, because my father's business was harvesting and selling the gum that was used in making opium.

My mother and aunt had grown fond of one another when they lived at Grandma's, and then, when they moved to their new home, which was a duplex, my mother began looking after my aunt. They were the same age, and they had been the brides of my grandmother's house. They were referred to in this way because in the old country tradition the bride, or *harss*—as she was forever after called—had to travel to the home of the groom. It was not uncommon at that time for four generations to live under one roof. Because my mother had so much energy and was no doubt eager to please and to make a place for herself in this new home, and because she was kind and loving by nature as well, she was eager to help my aunt. So my mother would cook if my aunt was unable to cook, and wash if she was unable to wash, and every day she brought my aunt fresh water from the well before my uncle came home, and the members of the family would say, "Everything has turned out for the best since they moved to their new home. Lousapere is growing stronger day by day."

And my uncle was satisfied. He would say, "Everything is very nice now. Very nice!" Years later, in the midst of our great troubles, when my aunt and I were alone, adrift and homeless, she would say to me, "No matter how much I do for you, Veron, it cannot be too much. I can never repay your mother." She worried about me. She cared for me. She loved me like a daughter.

I was always grateful that it was my aunt Lousapere who moved with our family to the new house, and not my aunt Arousiag. I often heard members of our family gossiping about her, and I was so grateful that she was not living with us, because ours was a happy home and she didn't sound like a happy person to me. She was very pretty, but also very spoiled. Her mother and father lived close by, and I overheard the members of our family say that she was always running home to her parents. This was a big disgrace, especially since our family and the Tehbelekians were the two wealthiest families in Azizya, and had, therefore, to set an example.

I was the first child born into our family. Soon after, my sister, Yeghisapet, was born, followed by my brother Apkar and then my brother Harutiun, who was just a baby when I was five years old and we moved to our new home.

Yeghisapet and I had one doll between us. It was a smooth-faced, beautiful doll, and we were very intent when we played with it. We would dress it, undress it, scold it, tease it, hug it, put it to bed, wake it up, change its clothes, teach it manners, etc., and all this without ever a fight between us.

My father was very different from my mother. He was frail, and fair-skinned, and almost always silent. He was a businessman, and highly respected. He would travel over the country with the gum we harvested from our poppies or with mohair, which he also sold, and he would return with big sums of money.

We always looked forward to his return, because every evening, when he was at home, he would play the *saz* (a small string instrument), and my mother would cook something special, and we would all be together, eating and laughing, and everybody would be happy because Father was home.

Father always brought home gifts for everyone in the family. When he came into the house, we'd run up to him and shout, "Papa! Papa!" but he wouldn't give us our presents right away. He liked to tease Yeghisapet and me. He would grab our doll and throw it up on a high shelf where the bedding was kept, so we couldn't reach it, and then we would start screaming. And my mother would say to him, "*Ouff*, why are you teasing them again?" and she would take it down, and we would start playing again. Our presents would be forgotten for the time being, and the next thing we would hear would be music coming from the fireside, where my father would be sitting, playing his *saz*.

These were the warm evenings of home that I shall never forget.

Our newly built one-story stucco home had French doors and a hallway that divided the house in two. It had wrought-iron windows and a slanted, red-tile roof. All the homes then had mud floors, which were broom-swept daily. The poor families were able to afford only straw mats, but the richer families had Oriental rugs. A new church was also built in the

Armenian quarter at the time, and this was where we went to school. I had been baptized in Aksehir because we didn't have a church in Azizya when I was born.

Aunt Lousapere and Uncle Apraham, who was my favorite uncle, and my cousin Hrpsime lived on one side of the hallway, and we lived on the other. Each family had three rooms: living room, bedroom and kitchen. The bedding would be taken down at night, and all of us would sleep in one room. In the morning the bedding would be aired out and put away. We had outhouses then and a large garden that our families shared. We would alternate the crops in our vegetable garden, and I remember that during our last summer there we had put in melons of all kinds, including watermelons. Our well was also in the garden, which had a high wall around it for privacy and protection. The poppies were grown beyond the garden walls, where I often watched the workers during the harvest season.

Each neighborhood had a bakery where everyone took his food to be cooked. A family had a prescribed time, and the bakery in Azizya was busy night and day. When the mothers or their children returned for the food, they would pay the baker a small fee for his services. We kept a charcoal fire in our yard and would take in a few of the red coals and place them in our *mangal* (a portable fireplace), which was stationed in the center of our living room. We would sit around

6

it and warm our feet, and it was around this fireplace that we ate during the cold winter months. The little cooking we did at home was done in ceramic kettles over an open fireplace. We often had *pilaf* (steamed rice or cracked wheat) and a meat-vegetable dish at night, such as *dolma* (stuffed vegetables) or *patlijan* (eggplant), and, of course, yogurt, which we had with nearly all our meals. We sat in a circle and ate from a communal dish with polished wooden spoons and forks. You were to eat only what was in front of you—no reaching! We sat on pillows, called *minders*. I can still hear Grandma admonishing us youngsters, "Fold your legs under you! Be civilized!" Then, this accomplished, she would add, "When a girl dies, the ground must approve; while she lives, the public must approve."

In the mornings, for breakfast, we had tea and toasted bread. There would also be cheese and *soujoukh* (sausage) on the table and *choereg* (breakfast roll). We children loved to put marmalade on our *choereg*, but the adults ate it plain. The bread we commonly ate was called *somen hatz* (round bread). We always came home from school for lunch. My favorite luncheon food was poppy-seed butter spread on the round bread, with raisins sprinkled on top. This would be enough to satisfy me during our hot summer months. But our winters were as cold as our summers were sultry, and so we often had *tarkana* (yogurt soup), which my mother sprinkled with pepper, to make it extra hot. That and *manti* (meat dumplings) were my favorite winter foods. Grandma would have a hole dug just before winter, which she would pack with straw. It was to store ice. Then, when the warm weather came, she would carefully cover it, and when she had company, she would be able to serve *shureb*, a homemade fruit-juice drink with ice. Her company was always very pleased and flattered to have this special treat.

My sister was two years younger than I, but my cousin Hrpsime was my age, and we went to kindergarten together. There was a beam in the middle of the classroom, and at the top of the beam, just beneath the ceiling, the teacher had pinned different colored ribbons. We called the game that was played with these ribbons braiding. It was my favorite classroom game. The teacher would start by singing, and then we would all join in, and at the same time, taking hold of our favorite color—mine was always blue—we would wind in and out, making a beautiful varicolored pattern with the ribbons. We wore red smock uniforms with the initials "M" and "B" sewn on the front. The "M" and "B" stood for *mangabardez*, the Armenian word for kindergarten.

Our school was on the second floor, above the church. We had the churchyard to play in, and after school, those of us who lived in the Armenian quarter would go one way, and the children who lived in the Turkish quarter would go another. Sometimes Hrpsime and I would go to Grandma's house after school, and then we would walk with our school-mates who lived, like Grandma, in the Turkish section of town.

The moment Grandma saw us, she knew that we had displeased our parents again or that they had done something to make us angry.

"Come here, let me look at you," she would call from the doorway. "What have you done now?"

And I would start complaining. "My mother pulled my hair!" Hrpsime would never speak. If I made a sad face, she made a sad face; if I smiled, she smiled. I was the leader.

"So, she pulled your hair again!" Grandma would exclaim, making a sad face for my benefit. "May her hands be broken, how could she hurt you! Come, come, let me look at my little darlings. Will you eat some raisins?"

We would nod our heads and follow her into the house. We loved to go with her into the pantry, where all the foodstuffs were stored for our two families. It had a rich, heady smell, and we would look in wonder at the shelves and crocks and at the meats and cheeses hanging from the ceiling. There were *basterma* (dried meat) and sausage, and raisins and dried fruits, and jellies and nuts and sugar and coffee and honey and *lablabie* (dried chick-peas), and so many other things. Our eyes could hardly take it all in. It was always cold and dark in the pantry, and very mysterious.

After we had our treat, and Grandma had fussed

over us for a while, we went outside to play with the Turkish girls next door. Their names were Heidi and Hajijya. We liked to trade bread with them. Heidi always came out with a piece of *youka* (flat bread), which was like our *parrag hatz*, and I would say, "Oh, I'll go in and get some *somen*." Grandma would give me a slice, and I would run outside. Then Heidi and I would exchange—her white unleavened bread for a slice of my whole wheat.

"Let's play jacks," someone would suddenly shout, and that was the signal to hunt for the five perfectly sized stones each of us needed to play the game.

When Grandpa came home from his store, we went inside. But we had to be very quiet, because he was almost always silent himself, and he did not appreciate unnecessary talk. He would wash his hands and face, and Aunt Arousiag would bring him a towel. Then he would go sit on the pillows in his corner of the living room. Beside him, he kept a bird in a cage. It was a black and gray myna bird with red feet, called *keglieg* in Turkish. He would speak to the bird, and the bird would answer back. Then Aunt Arousiag would bring *mezas* (hors d'oeuvres) and *raki* (an anise-flavored clear liquor made from raisins). If we sensed that he was in a good mood, we would slowly come close, shaking our hips just slightly, so our dresses would sway and we would be noticed.

"Well, do you want a piece of *jashei peda* [downtown bread]?" he would ask.

It was white bread, the kind we liked best of all. "Yes," we would say in unison, without lifting our eyes from the floor. He would put a piece of string cheese or sausage on it, and that would be our treat.

Then he would go back to sipping his *raki*, eating his *mezas* and talking to his bird, while Grandma and Auntie busied themselves in the kitchen making supper. Grandfather rarely smiled, except when he talked to his bird. Then he would smile, finger his mustache and look off into space. Only my grandmother wasn't afraid of him. If he lost his temper, as he so often did, she would quickly admonish him by saying, "A quick temper is a form of insanity!"

We all sat down to supper except my cousins Mariam, Arshalous and Garabed. They were too small to eat with us. Grandfather wouldn't allow infants at the table. "There will be time enough to look upon their faces and consider their deeds," he would say scornfully, downing the last of his *raki*.

At our table, in addition to Hrpsime and me and our grandparents, there would be Uncle Hagop, the gambler, his sourpuss wife, Aunt Arousiag, and my unmarried uncles, Apel and Haig. Uncle Apel, who was very meek and quiet, would later read aloud from the Bible, after the table had been cleared and the dishes washed. His one great passion was raising roosters and entering them in the cockfights staged by the Turks. Uncle Haig, my youngest uncle, was quiet and intelligent. He was being trained as a book-keeper, to take care of the records of the family businesses.

We always stayed overnight when we went to Grandma's. That was part of the treat, because my cousin and I could then sleep on the same mat together and giggle and be silly. We slept downstairs with our grandparents, while everyone else slept upstairs.

As we began to get ready for bed, Grandpa would invariably say, "Are these talkers here again?"

Hrpsime and I would be under the covers, talking and laughing, waiting for Grandma and Grandpa to prepare for bed. First they would put on their night-gowns—and we would giggle; then they would put on their little caps—and we would giggle even louder (with our heads under the covers, of course).

"Stop your tongues," Grandpa would roar at this point.

But when they took out their false teeth and put them in a water glass, it was more than we could stand. We'd screech hysterically, no longer able to contain ourselves. This was the point at which we always got our first spanking. We'd quiet down for a while, but pretty soon I'd stick my head under the covers and go *ptttttttt*, and Hrpsime would erupt with laughter.

Grandma would come over, and after throwing off

our covers, she would give us each two or three good ones on our bottoms. "That's two," she would announce, which was her way of saying, "Two is all you get."

And after this all would be silence, until the first rooster crowed.

We often saw the *kaimakam* (mayor) at Grandma's. He was a good friend of the family, and he must have liked the Armenians because he had enrolled his daughter, Lehman, in our school. She was a few years ahead of us, so we didn't really know her, but she had become our idol. She was very pretty, but the thing that made her special was her bangs. Because none of us wore our hair that way, we became more and more envious of her, until one day, when our parents had gone out and left us alone, we cut each other's hair in imitation of Lehman's. Then, in a fit of daring, we stole some of my mother's henna and applied just a touch to our bangs.

We were in the garden playing when our parents came home. I guess they could see the change in our appearance all the way from the kitchen window, and they called us in at once.

"Veron, what have you done!" my mother screamed at me.

"Nothing, Mama, we were just—"

"You call this nothing?"

"The mayor's daughter, Mama—" But I never

finished my sentence. Suddenly my mother was hitting me, and Auntie was spanking Hrpsime.

"You should be ashamed of yourselves," Auntie said. "Only Turkish girls wear their hair in bangs. You have brought a disgrace upon our family."

I loved the poppies that grew beyond our garden wall.

The fields, as far as my eyes could see, belonged to my father. One morning Yeghsa and I got up early to see the sun rise and to watch the workers arriving in the fields. We had just walked to the end of our garden when we heard the horse-drawn carts coming from a distance, rattling over the cobblestone streets.

"Why do they wear veils?" Yeghsa whispered when the carts came into view.

"It's a custom," I whispered back, not knowing myself why Turkish women always wore veils, even when they were working.

We watched the women, in their baggy pantaloons and long-sleeved blouses, get down from the carts and walk into the fields. The men who had brought them drove off.

I loved watching the women at their work, singing,

calling out to one another and laughing, bending over
the poppies and making slits in the pods with their
small knives.

The orange sun shimmered on the horizon, high-
lighting the colored garments of the workers—purple,
black, orange and burgundy, against the pale poppies
that moved so easily in the breeze.

"Oh, Yeghsa, isn't it beautiful!" I sighed.

That afternoon Mother, Yeghsa and I had a picnic
under our tree in the garden. Mother had brought
cheese and *lavash* (flat bread) from the house, and we
had cut open a watermelon from the garden.

"I saw you go to the edge of the garden this
morning," Mother said to us. Yeghsa and I looked at
each other. We had no idea that she had seen us.

"You mustn't touch the green balls; they are
poisonous."

"They were cutting them, Mama, and something
milky came out," I replied.

"That milky substance congeals in the night, and
the next day the men workers come, collect it and
form it into balls. These are the balls that Father takes
with him to sell."

"They look like *peda* bread, Mama," Yeghsa said.

"Yes, I suppose they do."

"I love the seeds, Mama," Yeghsa continued.

"I see you stealing them from the jar where I keep
them to sprinkle on our *choereg* before I bake them,"
Mother said, and reached over and pinched my sister's bottom.

"What else, Mama, what else do poppies give us?" I asked.

"They give us an oil that we use in cooking, and with the leaves we make a salad sometimes, but best of all is the *kashkash* we make from the seeds."

Easter was my favorite holiday. We would celebrate for two or three whole days. Mother would make blue and pink dresses for Yeghisapet and me. We'd color our eggs with onion skins, after they had been cooked, and then, selecting what we considered our strongest eggs, we would go to the schoolyard and have contests. If you said to someone, "I challenge," the other person would hold his egg in his fist, with the tip just showing between his thumb and forefinger, and then, with the pointy end of your egg, you would hit down gently on his. You had to crack your opponent's egg without cracking your own—and both ends of the egg had to crack before the "defeated" egg was turned over to the victor.

Our family always had a big feast on Easter—at Grandmother's, of course, because that was where we always went on holidays. As soon as we got inside the door, we would say, in greeting to each person there, "Christ is risen from the dead," and each would answer, "Blessed be the resurrection of Christ." We'd go into the living room and kiss the hands of our elders, one after the other. Then all the children would be given goodies—and sometimes money as well. Grandma would take us into her pantry, making a big ritual of it.

"So, what will it be, my little dears?"

"*Lablabie*," Hrpsime, who loved the dried chick-peas, would blurt out, unable to restrain herself.

Mariam always asked for *loukhoum* (jellied candy). That was her favorite.

"What do you want, Yeghsa?" I would ask, because she was so shy around Grandma.

"I don't know."

"Would you like *halva*, or *rojig* [grape-walnut rolls] or *lablabie*, or what?"

No answer.

"*Loukhoum*, like Mariam?"

"What are you going to have, Veron?"

I loved *halva*. "I think I'll have *halva*."

"I want *halva*."

The little ones—Arshalous, Garabed and Apkar—would hang back, but Grandma always brought them forward, and to each of them she'd say, "Let me see your hands," which each would immediately extend and always palm up and wide open—especially Apkar, who'd extend *both* hands. And then she would give them some goodies, too.

The important thing about Easter was church! No all the children loved church, but I did. Most of all loved the choir. Their voices never seemed to me to be theirs alone. I used to feel that Father God, as we called Him, was present everywhere in the church but I especially felt his presence in the voices of the

18

singers. I loved their white robes with the big red cross in back and the way they bunched together in front of the choirmaster, who motioned their voices forth with his right hand. I would suddenly have this image of the storks and their babies, who often made their nests on our roofs. Some people said babies came from storks, but I didn't think so. I was sure we all came directly from Father God. I didn't think I came from my parents. I believed I belonged to God, and He belonged to me. When I saw the storks feeding their little ones, and when the choir would lift up their voices to the sky—like the tiny beaks of the baby birds—I would feel my presence in their voices, trying to reach back up to Father God in Heaven.

The Easter season began with Parkendagh, the great feast day that was celebrated on the Tuesday before Lent. Grandpa would slaughter a lamb, and we would have shish kebab with pilaf, as well as all kinds of hors d'oeuvres and desserts. Then Lent would begin, to last for forty days, in which neither fish nor meat could be eaten. On Easter Eve the fast would end with an elaborate meal. During Lent we would go as a family to church every morning and evening to say our prayers.

I loved the holidays because it meant going to Grandma's. I felt closer to her in some ways than to my own parents. Even if I didn't always understand her words, I understood the feeling that passed between us, and this made me remember the words long afterward. She knew that I would often get tired of looking after my brothers, and even my sister, because I was the eldest. Although I was only seven years old, I already had many responsibilities.

"How pretty your children look together, Aghavni," she would say when we arrived at her home. "See," she'd say, looking straight at me, "you are not just daughters, you are also sisters. That makes you *twice* as strong. One hand cannot clap, but two hands can make a sound."

One of the last things I remember Grandma saying to me before our happy life came to an end, I have never forgotten. It was so sad to hear her talk this way, but somehow it made me feel grown-up, and there was something in the sadness that was happy too.

I had gone to her home one Friday by myself, and since there wasn't any school on Saturday, she walked me home in the morning. It was a crisp autumn day. The sky was cloudless, and in the distance could be heard the cries of the muezzin, calling the faithful to prayer. The streets were crowded with people: the youngsters running and playing; the elders shuffling along, fingering their beads.

"Let's sit a moment," Grandma said when we had come to a building that was under construction. We took our seats on two large facing stones.

We had been sitting in silence for some time when suddenly, I heard myself saying, "Grandma, I wish everyone could be cheerful."

"Why do you wish that, Veron?"

"Papa and Grandpapa hardly ever talk, and they seem so sad. Why, Grandma, why do they seem so sad?"

"Because God has given every man a sorrow, just as He has given every tree a worm. Only a grown thing can know this because it is something that can be revealed only with time."

"I don't think I'll ever be gloomy, Grandma, because I always like to see what's good. I don't let sadness enter me."

"I have noticed that about you. You see only what is pleasant. There is a meaning in this, and someday it will be made known. For now, it is one of life's secrets—one of God's secrets. Why you are one way, for example, and Yeghisapet is another. Everyone born is different. Everyone! God does not repeat Himself."

"I would like everyone to be happy—and to be good!"

"I hope you are as strong as you are hopeful, my dear. I think you are, or will be—should the time come for it to be necessary."

Grandma always talked to me as if we were the same age. One day I asked Mother about this. She said that I was Grandma's favorite grandchild because I was the firstborn child of her eldest son. That was when she told me that Grandma had had three daughters, in addition to her five sons. All three girls had died in infancy. The eldest was named Veron, and that was how I came to have my name.

Grandma was deep in thought, and I wasn't sure we were going to talk anymore, but all of a sudden she said, "I hope sadness never comes to you, Veron, but no one can read what has been written on another's forehead." Then she became quiet, but before long she spoke again. "You have a gay spirit and a generous heart; you take after your mother."

"I do?" I had hoped she would say that I took after her. I wasn't my mother's favorite. She liked my brothers best.

"What was your mother like, Grandma?"

"I'm always telling you things that I hope you will remember. I know you will forget much of what I have told you, but I also know that you will remember *some* of it—such as today's conversation, for instance. So, I would like to tell you something about my mother, especially a saying of hers that has meant the most to me in this life. She used to say, 'It is important to have peace in old age.'"

"I thought everyone had peace in old age."

"Only a few people do, because although peace is intended for old age, it must be earned and acquired before one has grown old. It must be *prepared* for."

"What's the best time for preparing, Grandma?"

"Responsible age."

"What's responsible age?"

"That's 'not yet,'" Grandma said, and laughed. "As far as you're concerned, I mean."

"I don't understand you, Grandma."

"In that case, let me say one more thing you won't understand. It is another of my mother's sayings, and it is something we can both ponder. 'What you learn in childhood is carved on stone; what you learn in old age is carved on ice.' "

"Can we go home now, Grandma?"

"Of course, darling. I'm sure they're wondering where I've been keeping you."

We began walking along in silence, and all of a sudden I started missing our kittens. Yeghsa and I used to put little cotton earrings on our kittens, and when they shook their heads, the little cotton balls would jiggle.

"Grandma, tell me about the time Tekyoos saved Papa's life and Mama burned her hand."

"What made you think of that, Veron?"

"Our kittens."

"Umm . . . well, as you know, your parents don't have a barn, and so when your father returns from his journeys, he always drives his horse and wagon to our place. For some reason, as soon as he gets to the stream by the Margarian house and crosses the little wooden bridge there, all the neighbors' dogs start barking. That seems to be how Tekyoos knows that your father is coming home. As soon as Tekyoos barks and runs to the door, Grandpa opens it and says, 'Benyat's coming! Go get Benyat, Tekyoos!' This one morning your father went to work with a bad cold. We tried to stop him, but he wouldn't listen to us. He's stubborn, just like you! When he started for home in the evening, he had chills and was running a temperature. Fortunately, the horses knew the way. Your father had covered himself with his coat, and at some point—nobody knows when—he fainted. So the horses brought him home, but when he didn't come down from the wagon, Tekyoos ran from the barn and started scratching on our door."

"I always forget the name of his sickness, Grandma."

"Your father had pneumonia. We were very worried because he is so thin and delicate. Most people who get pneumonia live only five or six days.

"Uncle Haig went to Smyrna and brought back a doctor who put your father on a special diet: *gatnabour* [rice pudding]; soft-boiled eggs; steak, cooked very rare; *choereg*, milk and wine. Only nourishing foods. And he said to me, 'Your boy is going to live. He'll never get sick again. He'll die on his feet.' "

"How did he know, Grandma?"

"Doctors know, darling; they can tell many, many things, just by looking at you. He did something to increase your father's fever, which helped him, though he was very sick for a long time. He used to jump out of his bed from delirium."

"And the doctor stayed with us until one day Mama saw something and burned her hand?"

"That's right. Your mother was outside. She had just taken down the wash and was coming in when a saint appeared before her and told her Benyat was going to live. You were at home, do you remember?"

"I remember she had very strange eyes. She walked into the room and put her hand on the stove. I screamed, 'Mama, Mama, you're burning your hand,' but she didn't hear me, and she didn't feel the stove. She just kept saying, 'He's going to live! He's going to live!' How did she know, Grandma?"

"Some people can see into the future."

"How?"

"Nobody knows for sure. It is one of God's gifts. Several of us in the family have it, but none as strongly as your mother. Well," Grandma said, looking up, "I see our story has carried us all the way home."

Sure enough, we were home. Yeghsa came running to meet us, clutching our doll. "Veron, Veron, one of the kittens ran away in the garden, and no one can find her."

"I have to go now, Grandma," I said, trying to be respectful and not show my excitement because I was dying to run and play with my little sister and be silly again.

Once a week a cry would echo through the house: "We're going to the Turkish baths!"—my grandmother, my two aunts, my mother, and Hrpsime and I. Mother and Aunt Lousapere would dress us in white, and then we would set out on foot, carrying our bundles, which included fluffy white towels, clogs inlaid with mother-of-pearl, *peshdimbals* (wine and ocher striped sheets of fine silk), a golden pitcher for pouring water, oranges for us, and for the adults pickled cabbages, called *tourshi*, which would be eaten after our baths.

The preparation, the excitement, the thrill of walking down the street with the women of the family—with Grandma leading the way: proud, dignified, looking neither to the right nor the left, assuring us that not a single Turk would dare look our way—were what made Hrpsime and me love going to the baths.

The woman in the entrance hall, opposite the fountain in which the goldfish swam, always greeted us with smiles and compliments, inquiring after the health and well-being of our family. Grandma did all the talking, and after the ceremonious exchange was completed, we would go to our quarter and prepare for the bath. Each *hamam* (bathhouse) had a manager. During the day, when the women, young girls and boys bathed, it would be a woman; but in the evenings, when the men used the baths, it would, of course, be a man.

Then we would get ready to go into the "hothouse," as Hrpsime and I called it. We would put on our *peshdimbals*, which tied around our hips and extended to our knees, slip into our clogs and walk proudly into the baths.

But once we were in the "hothouse," we no longer liked it. It was too hot. It was too noisy. There were too many boys, playing games and screeching. Not to mention all the fat ladies, with their mounds and folds of heaving flesh. We would all gather by the water, and we would just have to sit there. And then they would bathe us ... oh, how they bathed us. They used *loofahs* and they scrubbed and scrubbed. Hrpsime and I used to scream and cry and plead, but they went right on with their torturous scrubbing. This would be done not once, but twice! Then they would put some powder in our hair and send us back to our resting room, so they could bathe. Later we would have to go back. Somehow, we always managed to forget that we had to go back. And when they came for us, we'd beg not to be taken for another scrubbing in that hot, steaming room, with all the fat women and screaming boys. "No!" they'd shout over our protests. "You're not clean!" And back we'd go. After this, our entire bodies ached. They even washed our hair again. And then turbans ornamented with beads and lace were put on our heads. Back in our quarters, we were given oranges, while the grown-ups ate pickled cabbages. Then we rested, enjoying, *finally*, the luxury of the baths.

The very last ritual was the pouring of water over the feet. The grown-ups would do this for one another and say, "Let this be the water of health." To which the reply was: "Health be yours."

And then we'd go home.

In the evening, when Father came home, he would say to me, "So, did they take you to the baths again?"

"Yaaaaaaa," I would reply forlornly, sighing and looking down at the floor.

"How much did they bathe you—very much?"

"Very much, Papa; very, very much!"

"Let me see what they have done," he would say. "Let's have a look at you."

"I'm sore," I would cry, "I'm sore all over."

"Those bad ladies!" he would say, and make a face that was half smiling-teasing and half sympathetic.

Suddenly my seventh year came to an end.

The next year would be the longest year of my life.

This was the age at which girls began to learn different kinds of handiwork. The older girls were busy with their hope chests, and our mothers would send us to one or another of them to learn the different crafts and homemaking skills.

It was summertime, but the endless freedom of summertime games had come to an end. We could still play games, and wander in the garden, and go to Grandma's, but now there were allotted times for these things. If I put on a long face when Mother gave me a task, she would say, "Whatever you do, Veron, you do for yourself." But her advice, which I appreciated only later, never improved my mood.

I had never thought about time or change. But slowly changes began to occur. Our lives went on as before, but now our days, which had always seemed to be lit by the sun, were being shadowed by a dark cloud.

For the first time I began to sense the seriousness of our problems with the Turks. I had always known that they were not our friends, even though there were some with whom we were friendly, but now it seemed, in truth, that they were our enemies. We were Christians, and they were Moslems, but it was not this alone that separated us; we were also different in language, race and custom. We did live on the same soil, but I was told that soil could be owned and that the present owner of this soil, which we had always called home, was Turkey.

Grandma had hinted in the past that there might be trouble between the Armenians and the Turks, but now it was being talked about more openly—not only by her, but by everyone in our quarter. I was told that the Turks had massacred several hundred thousand Armenians a few years before, in 1895, and then again in Adana, in 1909, when I was two years old. And now there were rumors that there would be more massacres. I wasn't sure what all this meant, but I could see that the elders were worried. This made me worried, too, and I began to talk about my fears with the other children. No one could understand what was happening, but I could see that they were uneasy, too. This made me aware for the first time that our fears were not imagined, not childish, but real and deep-rooted.

I began to hear whisperings—at home and at Grandma's, especially at night, when my parents thought we were asleep. But more than their whisperings, it was the way they looked, the way they talked and moved about, that made me know something was wrong. I began to hear words like "deportations," "massacres," "annihilation." I didn't like the sounds of the words, but mostly I didn't like the looks on their faces when they said these words.

It was around this time that the Turkish army drafted my uncles Apraham and Hagop. When I asked Grandma about this, she said something about the World War.

It happened on a Sunday.

We were going to be deported—and now I understood what "deportation" meant. We were given three days to gather together our belongings and to leave. No one knew where we were being sent. People were giving things away, talking to each other in high-pitched voices, then breaking down and sobbing. I no longer remember the sermon at church that Sunday, only the sorrow in the priest's voice that he was unable to suppress.

At first I wanted to ask questions, but what was happening was just too terrible. I made myself believe that everything was going to be all right. I prayed to myself, and I tried to reason: Why should the Turks be doing this to us? Why should they drive us away from our home? But I couldn't find the answer, and so I prayed to Father God to deliver us from this evil and to deliver me from my own confusion.

I had to look after the children while Mother packed and took care of last-minute details. It was all a blur of anguish and excitement and fear. Grandma was at our home every day. Because she had given two sons to the Turkish army, she was not being deported. But Grandpa was. My aunts didn't have to go either, because my uncles Apraham and Hagop were in the army, and Hrpsime would also be staying behind. I wanted my aunt with us, and at the same time I was jealous because Hrpsime didn't have to go on our "march," as I had heard some people begin to call it.

On Friday Father went to Grandma's and got our horse-drawn wagon, and we began to load up for our journey. We took bedding materials and cooking utensils and a few other bare necessities. I also noticed that Father had bought packs and knapsacks, and I wondered why we would need them since our wagon was big enough for all of us to ride in. I saw that Father had harnessed our two strongest horses. We had already delivered all our precious items to Grandma's house for safekeeping while we were gone. Did this mean we would be coming back? This was a topic no one was willing to discuss. But we couldn't just leave these things in our homes, which everyone said would not remain unoccupied while we were gone. Hrpsime and Aunt Lousapere had already moved in with Grandma.

After we had loaded up, we went to Grandma's, so we could spend our final night together as one family. The next morning all the Armenians of Azizya who were not exempt were to appear in the town square. It was the saddest supper I had ever eaten. Finally, gathering us together, Grandma spoke. "However we may be dispersed," she began, "we are one family. If one of us should die, something in all of us will die, and if only one of us lives, then some part of each of us will live. Fortune cannot be built on misfortune. What the Turk is doing is mad; we must pray that we will not also be driven mad as a result—as victims of this aberration that has taken hold of them. For ourselves, we must never give up our hope and belief in life, or our faith in God. There is luck that brings ill, and there is ill that brings luck. Let us wait and see which of God's doors will be opened to us." She paused and looked at each of us in turn, before continuing. "This home and our fortune are safe, for now, and in this we are luckier than most. The road that leads away may also lead back. In our darkest moments this thought will be a comfort to us. If you escape, we will join you; if not, and you are able to return, we will be waiting here."

I didn't understand much of what she said, but her final words touched me very deeply. I was now better able to accept the fact that Grandma wasn't coming with us, and I was determined to return.

That night I don't think anyone slept. In the morning, Grandpa and my uncles Apel and Haig put their belongings on the wagon, and then began the long farewells. No one could hold back their tears. I had never seen Grandma cry before. She wasn't shaking and moaning, like some of the others, but tears were rolling down her wrinkled cheeks. I just couldn't say anything to her, and then, all at once, I started crying, too. I ran up to her and hugged her, and I wouldn't let go. "My darling child," she kept repeating, over and over, "God will return you to me, I know."

I don't remember the other good-byes. When I looked back, those we were leaving behind were standing in a line, with their arms raised high: Grandma, Aunt Lousapere, Hrpsime, Aunt Arousiag, who was holding Garabed in her arms, with Mariam half hidden behind her. I had never felt such love for my family before. At that moment something in me changed. I realized that I must begin to care for my sister and brothers in a way that I hadn't cared for them before. I began to know what a family meant.

I had fallen asleep. When I opened my eyes, I saw before me a brand-new world. Everything around me was new. I had only seen Azizya before, and now it felt as if I were suddenly in another country. For a moment I forgot the conditions under which we were traveling. We were passing out of a long plain, and in the distance was a beautiful mountain, which Father quickly told me was named Sultan Dagh. There was a train in the distance, heading in the opposite direction—the first train I had ever seen. I kept staring in wonder at everything around me, and before I knew it, we were on a causeway approaching a marsh through which a large stream ran. But when I looked back, I saw a long line of people, following behind us: a black ribbon of refugees, their heads bowed, many of them with babies strapped to their backs.

"Let me hold you up, Veron," Uncle Apel said, "so you can see Lake Aksehir." Uncle Apel was touched by my excitement, and he began to smile.

Yeghisapet was talking to our doll, and I could see she was trying to explain to the doll what we were doing in this wagon and why we were on this journey. My brothers were both lying down and looking very sad. It made me feel guilty for a moment for feeling so good, and so I crawled over to them and tried to cheer them up.

After a while Uncle Haig called out to Father, who was driving the wagon, "Benyat, according to the sign saw awhile back, this must be Aksehir we are approaching. Isn't it the birthplace and burial site of Nassredin Hodja?"

"Yes," Father called back, "this is the town. I had occasion to visit his sepulcher once, several years ago."

At this Grandpa's ears perked up, because Nassredin Hodja was his favorite storyteller, and he knew more of his tales than anyone in the family. Normally, he would have told a Nassredin Hodja story; but his smile quickly turned into a frown, and he didn't open his mouth.

There were beautiful gardens around the city, and I was hoping we would stop there, but we kept on going. We would stop, Father said, when the gendarmes told us to stop, and not before.

At night, when the gendarmes had given their signal, we would come to a halt, and the people would pitch their tents and cook some food. Our wagon was big enough for all of us to sleep in, but to avoid crowding, all the men but Grandpa slept under the wagon. The gendarmes woke us early in the morning and pushed us back onto the road.

During the afternoon of the fourth day I saw a line of walls in the distance. I heard Father tell Mother that these were the walls of Konya, which was once the capital of the Seljuks. It was a long time before we actually reached the walls themselves, which grew larger as we came closer. This was the first time I had seen a walled city, and I was fascinated. I liked the square towers, and I was hoping to see people in them; but they were all empty.

"Who's buried here, Papa?" Yeghisapet asked. Father turned around and smiled, and suddenly every one laughed in a kind of hysterical relief.

"As a matter of fact someone *is* buried here," Father said. "Do you see that bright green tower in the distance? Well, that is the burial site of Hazret Mevlana Rumi. He was the founder of the Mevlevi Dervishes."

"Who are they?"

"They are the Whirling Dervishes."

"Why are you telling the little ones about other religions?" Mother said, interrupting Father.

"Because they are young and their minds are still open. With all that is terrible in the world, let them hear also of what is good." Father turned around and looked at Yeghsa and me. "Are you listening?"

"Yes, Papa!" we said, excited by the prospect of a story.

"The founder of the Whirling Dervishes was Hazret Mevlana Rumi, a poet. They are known as Whirling Dervishes because that is the rite others identify them with, but they are actually a religious group."

"Why are they called Whirling Dervishes?" I asked.

"There is a ceremony, in which they put on high pointed caps and long white skirts, and to the accompaniment of a drum and flute, they dance, or whirl

heir eyes closed, their arms outstretched, with one
palm facing toward the earth, and the other toward
Heaven. They dance until they reach a state of ecstasy
in which their spirits achieve their desire to be united
with God."

Yeghsa and I became excited and started clapping
our hands. I was able to picture their dance in my
mind. Father looked at Mother and smiled. Suddenly
a thought came into my head that troubled me.
"Aren't the Dervishes Turks, Papa?"

"They were born Turks, of course, although their
founder was a Persian."

"Then they are Turks!" Mother exclaimed.

"Not exactly, although it is certainly true that they
are not *not* Turks. Men who love God love life. God
does not have a nationality, nor does life." Father
paused, but before continuing, he turned and looked
at me. "The Dervishes are Sufis, Veron; an ancient
religion, much older than Christianity."

"What else, Papa?"

"I'll tell you a story. Once, long ago, there was a
tradesman in a small village in our part of the world
who sat on his knees in his small shop, and with his
left hand he pulled a strand of wool from the bale
which was above his head. He twirled the wool into a
thicker strand and passed it to his right hand, and
with his right hand he wound the wool around a large
spindle. He worked in a continuous motion, and each
time his right hand spindled the wool, he said inaudi-
bly, *'La illaha illa'llah.'* [There is no god but God.]

37

There could be no abrupt movement or the woo[l]
would break and he would have to tie a knot an[d]
begin again. The old man had to be present to ever[y]
moment. We call this awareness. This is life. Su[f]
means awareness in life. As his sons grew, he taugh[t]
them his craft."

"So, what are they trying to say in this tale?[''
Mother asked.

"They are trying to say, 'Wake up!' They are tryin[g]
to say that we are unaware of the present moment—
that is, reality. All men's problems are caused b[y]
sleep. There is no such thing as conscious evil. Loo[k]
around you! The Armenians are asleep in thei[r]
foolish trust, and the Turks believe that two minu[s]
one equals three. Instead of being on this road t[o]
Hell, we should have escaped while there was time[.]
The man who is awake can read signs—the massacre[s]
of 1895, the massacres in Adana and Tarsus of 190[9]
and now the threat again in 1915."

"Are the Turks going to kill us, Papa?" I asked.

"No!" Mother quickly interjected. "We have [a]
wagon and money and treasures. Father will save us.[']

There was a long silence. I wanted to believ[e]
Mother, but I needed Father to confirm what she ha[d]
said.

We were about to enter Konya.

"This is a sacred city," Father said. "If we are t[o]
find rest and peace anywhere on our journey, it wi[ll]
be here."

38

When we entered the city, we began seeing all the deportees. There seemed to be thousands of them—some milling about the streets, others in camps at the side of the road. Many of them seemed unable to move, and I could see the lice crawling over their blackened clothes.

Without realizing what I was doing, I began comparing the way the deportees in the street looked with the way we looked, and for the first time I noticed how dirty we had become since leaving home. Our faces were red from the sun, which had baked the dirt into our skins. Our clothes and possessions were even dirtier than our skins.

A gendarme rode up to our wagon, and we came to a halt. Slowly, the caravan of people behind us moved to the side of the road and began to make camp.

"Do we have to get down, Papa?" I asked.

"Calm the children," Father said to Mother. "I'll

talk to the gendarme as soon as I can, and we will see what is to be done."

I watched our procession file off the road. I felt a great fear when I looked at the faces of the people, especially those who were our friends and neighbors, because they no longer looked like the people I remembered.

After a long time the gendarme rode up to our wagon and began talking to Father. They spoke for a while in low voices. I was unable to make out what they were saying. Then we started up again and began following the gendarme, but we were going off by ourselves, leaving all the others behind. I wanted to wave to the other people as we went off down the street, but nobody seemed to notice that we were leaving.

Slowly, we wound our way through the town, and then, all at once, we came to a park that was situated on a hill, and as we ascended, we could see the city all around us. There were a few other wagons scattered on the hill, and there were children outside the wagons playing.

After halting our wagon, the gendarme rode back and began talking to Father. This time I could hear what they were saying. "I have kept my promise to your mother by bringing you safely to Konya," he was saying, "but now I must return and make my report to my *kaimakam*. We have fallen on evil days, *effendi*, what can I say to lighten your load? May we meet again in Azizya after this present storm has passed."

"If we do not pass away with the storm as well."

"*Insallah!* [The will of Allah be done!]"

"Here," Father said, and thrust a small purse in his and. "Tell my mother that you have performed our amily a great service and that we have arrived safely Konya."

"Allah be with you, my friend," he said, and rode uickly off.

We got down from our wagon. Mother told me to ok after my brothers and sister while she prepared e evening meal. My uncles had gone off to gather rewood, and Father announced that he was going to lk to the men in the other wagons.

Later that evening, after we had eaten and Mother ld us children to get in the wagon and get ready for ed, I saw five men walking toward us from the other agons. They greeted Father and Grandpa, who took ut cigarettes and passed them around, and after all e cigarettes had been lit, they sat down around the re and began smoking in silence. Finally, one of the en began to speak, addressing Grandpa. "Konya is e dispersal center for the Armenians of the western rovinces," he began. "Our own people have already een sent off, but those of us, like yourselves, who ave had the means have been able to buy a little me. Most of us will join the marchers on the road, ut there has been talk by some of striking out one."

"For what reason?" Grandfather asked. "And here would they go?"

"They feel that if they can get to the sea, they will be able to find a boat to Greece or Italy or England."

"England is the enemy, and Germany—and then Turkey," one man suddenly shouted, but the first speaker continued.

"However, all the southern roads are blocked. The Turks are determined to march us to the Arabian deserts, where we will surely perish."

"Few will get that far!" a man with a large mustache and round, dark face interposed. "The Kurds and armed peasants are sweeping down from their mountain hideouts, killing and robbing the defenseless processions, and raping the women. All this with the support and encouragement of the gendarmes who are supposedly committed to our safe passage."

"The Kurds have always been our worst enemies," said another man, who had not spoken before.

There was a sudden silence, and except for the fire from the coals that lit up the faces of the men, it was black, moonless night, with the stars in the sky seeming to be reflected by the lights of the city.

"We are defenseless because the men who have not been inducted into the army or mobilized for railway and road construction work are being herded together on the pretext of being taken to another town, but in reality they are marched to the outskirts of the city and slaughtered. This has been reported by persons who were taken for dead by the enemy but managed to escape."

"There is a frightening thoroughness and deliber

42

eness here that terrifies me," Father suddenly xclaimed.

"It is as I told you!" the man who had interrupted irlier said. "The cold and deadly hand of the Ger- an has organized all this. Germany wants us out of e way, as we alone are capable of guaranteeing onomic and political independence for Turkey in sia Minor. Remove us and you remove the industry d talent and intelligence on which this empire rests. he Turks mean to replace the Armenian with the erman, but they cannot, for we belong here and the ermans do not. I don't think the Young Turks are pable of admitting this to themselves, and the real ar in their minds, for which we are being victimized, between their not wanting to believe this is so, and senting us unto death because it is."

"What he says is correct," another man said. "I ave seen with my own eyes a German officer direct- g artillery fire on the civilian population."

"It was for what this famous Baghdad Railway gnified—the Railway now being used in the deporta- ons—that Kaiser Wilhelm II fraternized with Abdul amid after the massacres of 1895 and 1896."

"Yes, to connect them with their holdings in Meso- otamia."

"We all know that it has since been dubbed "The erlin-to-Baghdad Railway," Grandfather said.

"I would not put it past the Germans to enslave us their desert lands, should we survive the march."

I began to wonder what the desert was, and then I

remembered the pictures our teacher had shown us in school . . . but then I must have fallen asleep, because I had a sensation of feeling warm, and when I opened my eyes, there was the sun and its orange light shining in my eyes.

When I sat up I saw that everyone else was sleeping. Only Father was awake. He was over by some bushes, gathering kindling, and so I got down from the wagon and ran over to help him. When he saw me, he stopped and sat down on the grass, because he could see I wanted to talk.

"Papa, don't the Armenians have any friends any more?"

"Did you hear us talking last night?"

"Only until I fell asleep. Isn't it pretty at night, Papa, with the stars in the sky and the stars in the street?"

"Are you afraid, Veron?"

"I don't know. I think so! Are we going to be all right, Papa?"

"We're going to try. We're going to try as hard as we can. And in every way that we know how. We will have to take each day as it comes, because from now on, no two days are going to be alike. And today I have wonderful news for you! One of the men I was talking to last night is going to make arrangements with the Turkish bath nearby. All the women and children who are camped here will be able to go this afternoon, and tonight the men will go."

I was so happy that I don't think I even thanked

...pa. I ran as fast as I could to the wagon to tell
...ama and the others.

That afternoon, when we came home from the
...ths, Mama combed my hair, and gradually all my
...ars disappeared. The night before we had had a
...arm meal, and today a bath, and now we were on a
...autiful hill overlooking this city that dressed itself
... night in white jewels that looked like stars. "I wish
...randma was here, Mama," I said all at once.

Mama didn't speak, and then I felt her body shak-
...g, and I knew she was sobbing. I was sorry I had
...oken, but it seems I was always forgetting where
...e were, and what was happening, or what was
...pposed to happen to us. Mama stopped crying, and
...en she said again what she had been saying almost
...om the time we started on our march, "I wish they
...ould just take us where we are going and get it over
...th."

As soon as Mama finished brushing my hair,
...ghsa and I ran off to play with the other children.
...ke me, the other children had forgotten our prob-
...ms and only wanted to play; but if we screamed too
...ud, the adults would shush us and then look
...ound, as if expecting some trouble. Only one boy
...as sad. His name was Dikran, and whenever some-
...e spoke to him, he would look up and brush the
...ir away from his eyes, and start speaking like a
...own-up, in a voice that wasn't a child's voice,
...hough it wasn't a grown-up's voice either. I felt

sorry for him, and so I asked him why he was so sa

"My father doesn't want to leave Konya. He say that during the last massacres we didn't have ar troubles with the Turks. Nothing happened. Christia and Moslem have always gotten along, that's what h says. And so we don't want to go away. But we had leave our home and all our things, and all our frien are gone."

"Do you want to play?"

"No!"

"Maybe someday we'll all be able to go back to ou homes. My Grandma in—"

"I think I'll go see if I have to get ready for th baths," he said, and ran off toward his wagon.

That night the men had another conference, but didn't know about it until the morning. I was so tire I fell asleep right after we had eaten. I had manage to stay awake just long enough to see the stars an the lights. In the morning, Mama and Papa wer whispering at the other end of the wagon, and b straining, I could just barely make out what they wer saying.

"So what have the men decided?" I heard Man ask.

"Don't you know by now that nothing is eve decided in a discussion among Armenians?"

"But you said last night that many important issue were discussed."

"Discussed, yes, but our talks lack the kind

46

reality they must contain if we are to plan an escape. It's too late now to *discuss* why we are in this predicament, unless that knowledge also contains a solution."

"Does it, then?" Mama asked.

"No! With us it never does. And what I am about to say doesn't take us any closer to freedom either, but I think I have finally figured out why we are so theoretical or, as Mother puts it, why there are two political parties for every Armenian. It comes from not having a country of our own to run, and therefore, none of our theories is ever tested. We play at government the way children play at house."

"Then nothing has been decided?"

"Only that each man will go his own way, which is to say that nothing will be done, and whatever happens happens."

"*Insallah*," Mama said, mocking the Turkish saying.

"Yes, *insallah*," Papa answered, "as if we haven't had enough of Oriental philosophy and fatalism. Let's get up and prepare for the day. I will forward my plan to the others after we have eaten."

We had just finished our breakfast of fruit and bread and tea when Father gathered us all together and began speaking. "We all know by now that we are being deported to the Mesopotamian desert. It is not known with certainty if the Turk intends to exterminate us or merely remove us for the duration of the war. Since governments are always mad and

47

impossible to understand, it will be best if we pu
aside our theories and try to control our fears so tha
we can make every attempt to survive. Everythin
changes with time, and for now time is our only ally
We know that the Turkish and German government
are our enemies, and we should also know that th
espousals of friendship for our cause in the West ar
mere journalism, politics and sentimentality. Onl
their missionaries can be trusted to offer real help
Men of God are without nationality and shouldn't b
confused with the governments they are said to rep
resent. Remember this!" He paused and considere
each of us in turn before continuing. "Thus far every
thing has gone in our favor, but it will not be so eas
once we reach Adana, which is not as civilized a cit
as Konya. We all know of the massacres that oc
curred there just six years ago. Everything depend
on the humanity of the police and the native popula
tion. Right now we have certain material means, bu
because we have no rights, no court of appeal, every
thing can be taken away at any moment. Therefore
we must be cautious, clever, suspicious and careful c
our every move. All escape routes have been sealec
We will rest here another day or two before joinin
the other caravans. May the grace of God be with us.

didn't want to leave Konya. I was enjoying my new
friends, and I dreaded going back on the road. Mama
had kept busy with my brothers and Yeghisapet, but
Papa spent more time with me than he ever had
before. He told me stories about missionaries and
orphanages, and how to tell Turks and Circassians
and Lazes by their costumes: that the Turks who lived
in cities wore fezes, the religious Moslems wore white
turbans, and the peasants always wore baggy trousers. The different tribes could be distinguished by
the colors of the scarves they wore as belts. He also
taught me to recognize the different uniforms of the
soldiers. He said that all soldiers were cruel and not
to be trusted, but that some were worse than others.
Papa also said he would give me different lessons
every day, and I was to repeat to myself everything he
told me until I knew it by heart. He said this would
keep me busy and help keep my mind from wandering.

I don't know how many days went by like this, bu
one morning we carefully packed all our possession
onto the wagon, and along with some of the others or
the hill, we wound down through the narrow mud
walled streets of Konya and joined the caravans or
the outskirts of town. We came to the place where th
Armenians of Azizya and Afyon had gathered, and
we stopped there and waited. Eventually one of th
officers came and talked to us, and I saw Papa pu
something in his hand, but I couldn't tell what it was

The next morning we started out again. It seeme
different somehow, and then I realized what it was
everything had gotten very quiet and serious again.
had lots of questions, but I didn't think anyone woul
want to speak to me, and so, when Yeghsa wanted t
play with our doll, I was glad to join in our game o
make-believe.

For some reason Harutiun started crying. Apka
was trying to calm him down. Apkar had becom
serious and thoughtful, and although we didn't talk t
each other about it, we both sensed that we under
stood something that Yeghsa didn't. It was a secre
bond between us, that aided us in helping Yeghsa an
Harutiun.

"I feel you are more hopeful than the rest of us."
was Mama addressing Papa. "Why is that?"

"You are thinking of all the horrible stories w
have been hearing about tortures and starvation. I ar
sure they are true, but they are only a part of th

picture. Bad news travels ahead of good news. I have done business with the Turks for years, and I believe understand their temperament. They cannot stay interested in anything for very long. I am sure the government means to exterminate us, but the Sublime Porte is in Europe, and we are in the heart of Asia, where the will of the government is difficult to enforce."

Mama had an unsatisfied look on her face.

"We are alive; we have been allowed to keep our wagon. I am trying to say that time is on our side."

"You said yourself that we can't know from one day to the next what is going to happen."

"Yes, that is true, but I believe the worst is over. The deportations began in April, nearly five months ago. Apart from the waves of hysteria that have swept the land, much of the local people's interest in the massacres has been in confiscating properties, petty looting and the possessing of women and children."

"What are they doing to the children?" Mama's face suddenly got very red.

"I have heard that the youngest boys are circumcised and converted to Islam, and the oldest are sold into slavery."

I was having difficulty understanding what Papa was saying, but I could tell by the tone of his voice and Mama's nervousness that it was something very bad, so when Papa turned to look at us children, I pretended to be playing with our doll.

"And the women?"

"Those who are willing to convert they attach to their harems; those who will not, they rape—and then either murder or sell to the Arabs."

Suddenly Yeghsa and Harutiun started crying and asking for food.

Uncle Apel tried to hush them. "We can't take our food out now; we have to wait for the gendarmes to tell us when we can eat."

"But they let us eat only at night, and I'm hungry *now!*"

Grandpa was sitting next to Yeghsa. He reached into his pocket and took out a morsel of bread and put it in front of her mouth. When she opened her mouth to take it in, he said, "Quiet." Then he gave us each a piece of bread, saying, "Quiet, quiet," to each of us in turn, but it wasn't a command, it was like a blessing. After that we were silent for a long time.

I was enjoying the scenery, which was always changing, and most of the time I could stand in the wagon and go from one side to the other to take in all the new things, especially the orchards, with their changing crops: pomegranates, figs, nectarines, apricots, peaches. I wished that we could stop and pick some fruit, but I knew it was futile even to ask.

The second morning I saw some animals I had never seen before. Eight strangely silent camels were moving in a line, led by a very fat man on a donkey who was hanging, fast asleep, on the donkey's neck. A little boy, no taller than Yeghsa, was darting in and out between the camels, trying to keep them in a straight line.

"Where are the camels going, Grandpa?"

"I believe they are going to Smyrna. Is that not so, Benyat?"

"Yes," Papa answered, "they are carrying hides of wool to market."

"Weren't the camels strange, Grandpa? Why were they so strange?"

"Because they have been removed from their homes. They are the true inhabitants of the desert— creatures of sand and stars and silence."

"Why are desert creatures strange?" I asked, even more puzzled than before.

"Because all things that live in the desert *become* the desert. The desert has no need of man. It is nature contemplating itself, awaiting the decision of the stars."

We had left the orchards and mountain streams behind, and the landscape was becoming dry and barren.

"Look back at Konya, everyone!" Uncle Apel exclaimed.

"Yes, isn't it beautiful from this distance?" Uncle Haig replied. "I hadn't realized it was situated on an elevated plateau."

"An oasis in the desert!" Grandpa said.

"Is this the desert?" I asked.

"Not yet," Papa answered. "The real desert doesn't begin until after Adana. But this is desert enough for

53

now. We'll be coming to salt lakes soon, and the only trees we'll see for a while will be cottonwoods. It's going to get very hot."

"It will be excellent preparation for what is to come," Grandpa said.

"I'm thirsty," Yeghsa said. I was glad she had spoken up because I was thirsty, too.

Mama turned and looked at Yeghsa. She looked so sad and tired, and so very different from the way she looked when we lived in Azizya. "From now on we can have only one small drink of water during the day."

"Maybe the guards will let us stop if we come to a stream," Uncle Haig said.

"Not without payment," Papa answered.

"Is your doll thirsty?" Grandpa asked Yeghsa.

"Yes, very thirsty, Grandpa."

"Tell her we are going on a special journey that will be full of many surprises, for which a little thirst is a small price to pay."

Yeghsa began whispering to our doll, and in no time at all she was completely lost in her play.

I looked up at Grandpa, and we smiled at one another.

That night we went to bed feeling thirsty and hungry, but no one complained. We were getting used to having less, and of course we knew we were very fortunate because we had a wagon and could ride, while many others had to walk. The gendarmes didn't feed us that night, but I could see that most of the people had brought a little food with them. The next morning we had biscuits and fruit, and in the evening we had the same thing, except that Mama put a little piece of cheese on our biscuits. That evening several people came to us asking for help, and Papa gave each of them some flat bread he had been able to buy in Konya. After it had grown dark, I heard Papa telling some of the men who had gathered around our fire that he had spotted a Yuruk village in the hills just before we stopped.

"How do you know they are Yuruks?" one man asked.

"By the low-pitched tents and by their cattle herds. Did you not see the cattle?"

"Yes, and camels as well."

"The camels are also theirs."

"What is your intention?" Grandpa asked.

"When all here are asleep, I intend to sneak back to their encampment and bargain with them for milk and eggs."

"They are shrewd bargainers." It was one of the men from Konya who was driving the only other wagon in our caravan. "The Turks look down on the Yuruk women because they never cover their faces, and they are not afraid to interfere in their husbands' dealings if they feel they are being bested. You'll not have an easy time of it."

The next morning Papa looked tired, and when Mama fed us milk and eggs for breakfast, I knew the reason why. We were beginning to feel again the way we had when we arrived in Konya, though we weren't nearly as dusty or dirty.

That afternoon a few of the older people began to fall down, but the gendarmes wouldn't let anyone stop and help them. When the first one fell, Uncle Haig jumped up and tried to call to one of the gendarmes. "Let us take them, let us take them here," he kept saying, over and over.

"It's no use," Grandpa said, "I have already asked and been refused."

It was so pitiful to watch them lying there, one after the other, as our caravan moved on. After we had rounded a bend and they were out of sight, one of the gendarmes rode back, and soon we heard the sound of rifle shots.

"*Azatveren* [They are released]," Grandpa said without looking up.

"Next will come the Kurds," Papa said, "unless they are so fattened by plunder that they cannot move from their hovels."

The time dragged on, and I began to lose interest in the scenery. I slept as much as I could, so as not to think about what was happening to us or what was going to happen. But before long the scenery began to change, and we soon came to a river that Papa said was called the Chait Su. When Apkar looked up and saw the river, he began asking for water to drink. He was immediately joined by Yeghsa and Harutiun.

"Tonight we will drink," Papa said, "I promise you. I want all of you to start looking for the white bridge; let's see who will spot it first. I think we will be stopping there because beyond the white bridge are the Taurus Mountains."

56

Several hours passed before the bridge came into ew. It was so beautiful that it was worth waiting for. saw it first, but Grandpa made a sign with his eyes, d I had to let Yeghsa see it first, so Papa could ngratulate her. It was made of white stones that ended with the shape of the road, which curved pward into a half circle that disappeared into the lds of the rocky hills. As we approached, I saw me donkeys and then a string of long-necked ani- als in the distance.

"Look, Yeghsa, camels!"

As they approached us, swaying and gurgling, I oticed they were carrying carpets, as well as huge les from which something white and fluffy was icking out. "What's that, Mama? The white fluffy uff, I mean?"

"Cotton."

"Cotton?"

"It grows near Adana. It's spun into yarn, and then oth is made from it."

How strange, I thought, fabrics made from some- ing that grows on trees. "On trees, Mama?"

"No, small bushes."

"How big, Mama, how big?" I asked excitedly.

"Maybe waist-high, and the cotton, when it breaks t, looks just the way it does on those bales."

I was fascinated, and I wondered who first thought making cloth from such small white balls of cot- n.

The next day we passed the most beautiful site I d ever seen. Papa said it was called the Cilician

Gates. It was a narrow gorge enclosed by high, very very high walls, which went straight up in a line on both sides.

"It's scary and exciting, Papa. I feel as if we're in tunnel, even though I can see the sky."

"It's almost as if nature created the gorge," Mam said, "so that man could behold her wonder."

The road got narrower and narrower as we approached the perpendicular walls. There was just enough room for the road and a clear mountai stream which flowed on our left, with its bed brightly visible polished stones. It grew dark an damp, and the only sound was the stream echoing i our ears, its rushing sound seeming to come from a directions at once.

Above the highest peaks, slowly circling back an forth across the open sky, were huge bare-necke vultures. The sight of them stiffened my already chilled bones, until the only sound I could hear wa my own breathing. We were all staring upward, bu no one uttered a word.

We crossed the top of the Taurus Mountains and began our descent before camping for the night. We could see for miles and miles into the valley, which Papa said was one of the most fertile farming regions in the world. It was wrapped in a golden haze, and Mama, pointing to the grayish shimmer on the horizon—far off to our right—told us it was the sea and that the silver ribbons in the distance were rivers.

"It is difficult to believe we are living in a time of trouble," Mama said, looking out over the vast and peaceful expanse.

"Or to understand why," Grandpa answered.

I wondered myself how I could ask this very question in a way that would bring an answer I could understand. If I asked Mama, she would get excited and either start crying or tell me to keep quiet. Papa was calm, but I didn't always understand what he was telling me; and Grandpa would either become sad or angry, changing the subject or avoiding it altogether. I decided I would try to remember what Papa said, so I could go over it later on and try to understand his explanations.

Great woolly clouds were drifting over the valley, casting their dark shadows on the earth, as we began descending the slopes. It seemed to be taking forever to reach the valley, even though it appeared almost close enough to touch.

"This air is becoming rich with the perfumes of nature and the moisture that gives it life," Uncle Haig said.

"That valley is as hot as Egypt," Papa said to Uncle. "Tomorrow we will long for the thin mountain air we are leaving now."

In the morning we began to pass tiny villages in the foothills, where Papa said the people of Adana came in the summer to escape the heat. The homes were built along the sides of the hills, and as we passed below them, the people came out and stood in long lines and stared down at us. We felt like insects at the mercy of creatures whose minds we couldn't read. The first line of witnesses watched us in silence, and I was relieved when they disappeared at the first turn in the road, but before long we came to another line of people, this time on the other side of the road. As we passed below them, I heard one man shout, "Infidel dogs." This prompted two young boys to pick up stones and hurl them at our procession.

We kept moving, down and down; the winding

oad, the lush green vegetation and the crystal, bel-
owing waterfalls—the first of their kind I had ever
seen—for the moment drowned out all else, including
even our fears and uncertainties.

The next day, as we approached Adana, we saw the
endless rows of cotton fields. It was the harvest
season, and men and women were everywhere, wearing identical baggy pants. They stopped their work
and stared at us, motionless, quiet, unbelieving.

"They are the peasant help brought in from the
surrounding hills," Papa said. "This is probably the
first caravan they have seen."

We could see Adana now, with its smokestacks
that Papa said belonged to the cotton factories. We
were diverted onto a side road, away from the main
road that led to the city, and for mile after mile we
passed through olive and fig orchards.

"Once again we are fortunate," Grandpa said. "The
fewer people we see, the better I like it."

We came at last to a river. "We will stop here," a
gendarme said, and with that all but one of them rode
off in the direction of Adana.

"This is the Seyhan River," Papa said, "one of the
rivers we saw from the mountains. It runs through
Adana and empties into the Mediterranean Sea."

We were hot and tired and dirty, but that evening
we bathed in the river; our first bath since Konya.
Mama was even able to wash some of our clothes.
We had very little food left, but we were so grateful

to be clean that we didn't mind being a little hungry
That evening, after supper, I saw Papa change his
jacket and then put on a fez. He walked quietly over
to the river and then started walking upstream in the
direction of Adana, disappearing among the trees.

Mama understood the troubled look on my face
"Don't worry, Veron, Father can pass for a Turk
anywhere. He'll be back with news and food either
late tonight or early tomorrow."

Papa came back to camp late that night, and in the
morning he surprised us with something that was
sweet and delicious, that I had never eaten before. It
was sugarcane. He brought other kinds of fruit as
well, and two loaves of fresh bread.

"I'm glad you thought of the sugarcane," Mama
said. "You have the little ones smiling again."

That night Papa left again. We couldn't find out
why we had come to this spot by the river, nor would
our guard tell us when we would be leaving. "I don't
think he knows himself," Uncle Apel said. "If anyone
asks him, he only says, 'Hurrying comes from the
devil, patience comes from Allah.' He is totally indifferent to our plight. We are to go to the river now
only once a day, to obtain water for cooking, when
we are also allowed to make our only fire of the day
No shouting or playing on the part of the children,
and the men cannot gather in groups of three or
more."

"It is the not knowing that ages a man," Grandpa

aid. "How long we will stay; where we are going; what will become of us in the end. All is unknown. Only the forbidden road of return remains alive in my heart, but like my heart, it is choked with broken weeds."

"I wish they would send us where we are going and let it over with," Mama said again, repeating what I had heard her say many times before.

All the next day Papa didn't return. I was anxious at first, but Mama told me not to worry. "He will return when he has obtained what he is looking for—and he has promised to bring more sugarcane!"

The next morning Papa was with us when I woke up. He was very quiet and serious, and this reminded me how different he had been since we left home. He was always raising our spirits and taking our minds off our worries. I guessed that this was Mama's job when we had a home, but now that we were homeless, it was Papa's job to look after us in this way. Anyhow, he wouldn't tell anyone what was on his mind. "I will speak of it tonight when we are allowed to gather and eat, and after the children have been put to bed," he said to Mama.

That evening, immediately after we had eaten, Mama told me to take Yeghsa and the boys back to the wagon and put them to sleep. Harutiun started fussing for Mama, so I sang him a lullaby, and pretty soon he and the others were fast asleep. I got down from the wagon very quietly and tiptoed back to the fire. All the men were sitting in front of the fire, in circle, with the women in back of them, and a few o the older children in back of the women. I sat dow by one of the older boys, who I knew would not giv me away.

The men were still speaking Turkish, and I won dered why the discussion hadn't begun yet when noticed the guard standing by a tree just beyond th fire. He was smoking a cigarette, and it was onl when he raised his hand to his mouth that I could se a portion of his face in the glow of the cigarette as "The fire is to be put out, the area vacated and a conversations must cease in one hour." He walked u to the circle, flipped his cigarette into the fire, turne and disappeared in the dark.

After a short silence one of the men said, "Pleas Benyat, speak. It is time you told us what you saw i Adana."

"It is in shambles," my father began, "tradesme craftsmen, businessmen, doctors—in short, all the A menians who kept the city functioning and money i circulation—are gone, and the Turk cannot manag his own affairs. The rabble—mostly Kurds and Ci cassians—are roaming the streets. The forces of lav cannot deal with the situation."

"Is this why we are being detained here?"

"Yes, I am sure of it. They cannot spare the gen darmes it would take to move us out."

"What is to become of us?" one of the women sai in a voice of despair.

"I believe the hysteria has passed. They have put much of the blame for whatever guilt they are feeling themselves on the Kurdish bands, and on the gendarmerie, which is composed of the lowest element of Turk. Most of the patrol guards, I have learned, are made up of released prisoners. The gendarmerie have not only stood aside while the Kurds robbed the caravans and defiled the women, but they have allowed the rabble of the towns they have gone through to loot and rape as well. In many cities the entire male population has been slaughtered. One hears of mounds of corpses scattered throughout the country, their bones picked clean by dogs and vultures."

"How many are dead then?" one of the men asked.

"The figure has been put at nearly one million, but no one can say for sure."

"My God, do they mean to exterminate us all?" someone gasped.

My father waited a long time before answering. "They want us out of the way, so they can fight against our allies."

"*Our* allies?" someone said.

"France and England on one side, and the Russians on the other. They are not unaware of our sympathies, or of the underground work done by our revolutionaries. Concerning this, I learned something about the 1909 massacres in Adana of which I was totally ignorant."

"What is that?" several men asked at once.

My father took a deep breath before he began
"After mingling in the bazaar, where I picked up bits
and pieces of information, I went to one of the
coffeehouses, hoping to get some news that would be
more official. At the entrance I saw something that
made the blood rush to my temples. Tacked to the
wall was a small card on which was printed a map of
Cilicia, with writing in Armenian. Above the card,
which was charcoal-smeared, and written over in a
crude hand, were the words 'What Armenia, infidel
dog?' I turned the card over and read, in Armenian,
'The Future Armenian Kingdom of Cilicia.'

"In the coffeehouse I saw a *mullah* [religious
teacher] sitting by himself in a corner of the room.
approached him, making the customary exchange in
Turkish, after which he asked me to join him for
coffee. As he motioned for the waiter, I explained to
him that I was a businessman from Afyon and that
was intrigued by the postcard I had just read on my
way in.

" 'Yes, one of our local hotheads,' he said, explaining the defaced card and scrawled message.

" 'But what does the card itself mean?' I asked.

" 'That dates from the 1909 troubles,' he answered,
and seeing that the puzzled expression did not leave
my face, he continued. 'As you know, when Abdul
Hamid was dethroned in 1909, the new government
of Young Turks promised certain freedoms to the
Armenians and other subject races. The Armenians,
in a burst of riotous folly, foolish even for them,

began shouting from their clubs and meeting chambers of the freedom that would soon be theirs. It was then that they sent those unfortunate cards you ask about through the mails, and marched through the streets bearing banners of Lesser Armenia. They even began speaking of a royalist army hiding in the mountain fasts of Hadjin and Zeitun, which was of course a bluff. When word came down from the government that the Armenians were to be slaughtered, you can imagine the vengeance with which the populace went at their work—and the atrocities that followed.'

" 'Still, that is nothing compared to what we have now, if I am to believe what they are saying in the market place.'

" 'It is most regrettable, most regrettable. Christian and Moslem have always been neighbors, if not always friends. The accusation that the Turk is persecuting the Armenians on religious grounds is the work of Western journalism. Until now not a single act of desecration had been committed against the Armenian church, but now ... what can we say, *effendi*, it is a disgrace.'

" 'It is difficult to find anyone who will speak of the atrocities. In my city it is scarcely mentioned,' I lied.

" 'Yes, I understand the Armenians have been peacefully removed from the western provinces, but here the butchery has been wholesale.'

"We were both silent for some time, but after the waiter had brought us fresh coffee and the *mullah* had taken a loud sip from his cup, he sighed and said, 'Aside from the blight on our conscience, it is a pity. Armenians are intelligent, talented and resourceful. I for one have never resented the control they have maintained in the financial world. After all, our people cannot plan and organize, and so all have benefited from the Armenian's acumen. Although divided by faith, are we not all Orientals? Cannot Greek, Armenian and Turk live in amity?'

" 'With us it was always so.'

"He continued as if I hadn't spoken. 'I have analyzed the problem. The Armenian began to align with the West—first slowly through the missionaries, and then through the instigation of their intellectuals who had gone off to France to be educated. They returned with notions of autonomy and other nihilistic ideas about "freedom," so that when the war came to our country, they were the natural dupes for the Western powers, who began using these poor, uneducated Christians as their excuse to heap invectives on our heads and to rouse their own masses against us, should they feel it necessary to go to war with our country. So much of it is outright lies. We have never been granted a fair hearing before the great tribunal of humanity. The Armenians are not alone in being victimized by our government; we are victimized, too. Ah, life is cheap, *effendi*, and we have always accepted the turn of the wheel—believing that death is a welcome release from this life. *Insallah!*'

"We sat in silence for a long time. As I got up to

68

leave, the *mullah* began speaking again, more to himself than to me. 'Ah, we have all been children,' he began, letting out a deep sigh of unhappiness. 'The Turk has been wicked, the Armenian childish. Or reverse the order if you like, but either way, you have a pair of fools, who together cannot accomplish this game called life in a single house—and so the child who thinks the house is his has expelled the child whose house it is surely not; but the poor Armenian child does not have a home to return to, or a neighbor who will give him shelter, and so he has been banished to the desert.' He paused for a long moment before continuing. 'There is but one land, and God is our only witness, and the earth our only dwelling place. Men would rather die than learn this simple truth.' "

The fire made a loud cracking noise. I peered over the shoulder of the person in front of me at my father, whose head was now bent forward, in a posture of silence. I began to crawl backward, slowly, in the direction of the wagon.

The days dragged on. Was it a week, two weeks, or even longer? I lost track of the days and even the month. Papa came and went, and we always had something to eat, but it was impossible to remain cheerful. Although one day followed another in regular monotony, we knew that the monotony might be broken at any moment, but that whatever came to break it was certain to bring something even worse in its wake. Papa said they were still deporting the Armenians from Turkey, and it was only a matter of time before they sent us to the Arabian desert. But to live in uncertainty was the worst thing of all, or so we all felt, and whatever our fate was to be we were anxious that it present itself.

All the love that was given me since we left home I had simply taken for granted, but I was no longer the child that I had been when we started on our journey. Something deep inside me, which I knew was love, was going out to all the people who were with us on our march. Everything was being shared; no one thought only of himself, but rather, it seemed as if each of us put the other person first. We all were trying to make the other person's load lighter, and for some reason this, more than anything we might have done for ourselves, made our own load lighter as well. I realized that without the children to be saved, the elders might not have found the reason to go on, and without the elders to guide us, we, of course, would have been helpless victims.

One afternoon four Turkish soldiers on horseback came bursting into our camp. They exchanged a few hurried words with our guard, who immediately gathered his few belongings, jumped on his horse and rode off in the direction of Adana.

"You have fifteen minutes to get your things together," one of the soldiers said. "Hurry! What you cannot gather will be left behind."

Several of the men grabbed up the canteens and flasks and rushed to the river, while the women began packing the knapsacks. Mama told me to throw our things in the wagon, while she rushed off to help some of the others.

"They are irregulars," I heard one man say to another, as they rushed off past me on their way to the river.

"The end of our journey is now upon us; we will be delivered, or we will perish—like dogs," the other said.

We were a caravan again, on the march. As soon as we came to a spot in the river that was shallow enough, we began to cross. The river's edge was bloated with varicolored leaves, and looking across the river at the nearly barren trees, I remembered how green everything had been the day we arrived. Some of the leaves swirled and moved heavily downstream, around our feet, while others sank and disappeared. We found a worn footpath on the other side of the river, and slowly began to wind our way toward a distant purple mountain, on which the sun shone for a moment before being covered over by a heavy gray cloud.

For three days we trudged toward that mountain, which seemed to grow farther and farther away.

"Are we going to Arabia, Papa?" I asked one day.

"Syria, darling, we're going to Syria."

"Is that where the desert is?"

"Yes, we'll come to it after we cross the mountain. But not right away; the real desert, where nothing grows, is still very far away from here."

"But where are we going?"

"I don't think anyone knows."

"A part of me rejoices that we will be leaving Turkey," Grandpa suddenly said, "but how can one look forward to being at the mercy of the Arabs?"

"Oh!" Mama exclaimed. I waited to hear what she was going to say next; but she fell silent, and I could see that no one wanted to speak, because there was nothing more to be said.

We were passing through many little towns on our way to the mountain. Some of the people stared at us,

ut most of them either looked away or ducked
nside the homes or buildings.

"They are sick and ashamed of seeing us," Mama
aid.

One man ran up to our wagon and tried to offer us
ome bread, but one of the guards rode up and
:nocked it from his hand. The man sat down in the
lust and would not move, though each of the guards
ode up to him in turn, prodding him to move, until,
nally, one of the guards spat on him in disgust.

"He is as tired as we are," Papa said. "There are
imes when one man alone must bear the conscience
or an entire village."

At last we came to the mountain. It wasn't nearly as
igh as the last one we had crossed, but it was more
han two days before we finally got to the other side.

"The farther we go, the poorer everything gets,"
Mama said. "Nothing can grow here, and even the
uman settlements are becoming scarce."

"It is the people, not the land, who are barren,"
'apa replied. "This was once the site of a great
ivilization."

"Mesopotamia," Grandpa said, quietly, to himself.

We had been heading south into hot, muggy
veather. We soon ran out of water, and our food
upply was very low. Papa was able to buy water at
he villages, but only when the guards were willing to
top for food or water for themselves. We were
topping to rest more and more often, and I didn't

know how the ones who were walking could go on. I tried not to think of all the people who were no longer with us.

On the morning of the third day after we had crossed the mountain we were met by a man on horseback who looked different from all the other guards I had seen, though I was sure he was either a soldier or a gendarme.

"We must be in Syria," Papa said. "That man is a Bedouin Arab."

We were told to stop and rest. Everyone was restless and agitated, unsure of what would happen next. Our march through Turkey had ended, but there was somehow no sense of relief. Everyone was talking about how uncivilized the Arabs were. "The future is uncertain," I heard one man say.

"And with the Arab, unpredictable as well," another answered.

Before long the Turkish guards rode off, on the road over which we had come.

"They have brought us to this no-man's-land and left us to die," one of the women said, and began whimpering.

"Get up!" the Arab guard said in broken Turkish. "You march Gatma on this road, and you stay," and with that he rode off in the direction that we would be traveling.

"Why has he left us?" I asked. It was the first time we had been left unguarded since we had lived on that hill in Konya.

"We won't need any help to make us move now,"

one of the women said. "That sun and this burnt earth are the only prodding we'll need from now on."

But nobody knew where Gatma was or when we would get there. Even Papa said that he had never heard of it. "It must be a very small village or town," he said at last.

That afternoon we passed through a very poor village where we were able to buy milk and eggs. We didn't like the looks on the faces of the Arabs, and as soon as we bought our food, we left. None of the people we spoke to knew Turkish. They were rude and unfriendly, and they frightened us. How can we live among such people? I thought. They are just too different from us. I began thinking about our home in Azizya with such longing that I almost started crying. I wondered how Grandma was, and if she was taking care of everything for us. Someday we'll go home, I thought. We just have to.

Toward sunset we came to another village where we were met by the same guard who had relieved the Turkish soldiers. He told us to march to a cluster of trees just outside the village and to make our camp there.

"Milk sell; yogurt sell; bread sell—you wait, womans come," he said in his broken Turkish. That night he came to our camp to talk to Papa, who was now our leader. Before he left, I saw Papa hand him some coins. Later Mama told me that Papa had to bribe him so he would protect us from the other Arabs, who wanted to rob us in the night.

"His job is done," I heard Papa say to Mama.

"Tomorrow we will be met by another guard. He has urged us to move on, as he says the rainy season is overdue, and once it comes, all travel and activity will come to a stop. He also told me that some provision has been made for us in Gatma—where we will be given tents and an area to camp in, among the deportees who are already there."

Papa got us up very early the next morning. There was a little light in the sky, but I could still see all the stars. "Get the children ready, Veron; we need to make an early start." I could see Papa was worried, and I remembered what Mama said about the Arabs wanting to rob us.

"Hurry now!" I heard Papa saying to the others. "With luck we'll reach Gatma tonight. We must get there ahead of the rains. We will stop to eat when the sun has risen in the sky."

That afternoon it began to drizzle.

"This will not slow us down," Papa said. "The earth is hungry for water and will not easily turn to mud."

But the rain continued, hour after hour.

"Take off your shoes and put them in the wagon," Papa shouted, and everyone quickly took off his shoes and passed them forward. "Gatma is just ahead!" he hollered back, after all the shoes had been collected.

Everyone was soaked through by the time we achieved our destination. It seemed like a miracle that we had actually arrived, because in the last hours our wagon was hardly moving at all, and the walkers were up to their ankles in red mud.

I shuddered when I saw the people in the camp. Everyone was sick with an illness that had changed his color, and people were dragging themselves back and forth from the area they were using for a toilet; but they were so weak that many of them were unable to push their way through the mud, and they were sitting and falling down, weak, exhausted, dying.

"Cholera," I heard Papa say, and I felt our wagon come to a halt.

I didn't think the rain would ever stop falling. Although we were given tents, it was impossible to get warm, and more than a week went by before the rain stopped long enough to allow us to make a fire and eat our first hot meal. What food remained in the camp was shared by everyone. There was a little flour for making bread, some cracked wheat and dried fruits, and very little else. If it weren't for the illnesses, there wouldn't have been any food left, but most of the people were too sick to eat, and many had already died.

We were given one of the empty tents that had been vacated because of the numerous deaths. After we had arranged our few belongings and tried to make ourselves a little comfortable, an elderly man came into our tent and began conversing with Papa.

"You are from what place?" the elder asked.

"Azizya," Papa answered.

"You started from Afyon then," he said, smiling.

78

vith us. You are Benyat Dumehjian. I thought I
cognized your wagon."

Papa was startled, as we all were, and stared at the
an without speaking.

"You left us in Konya; I saw you being led away by
gendarme into the city center. We wondered what
d become of you." After a short pause, while he
oked at all of us in turn, he continued. "Our hard-
ips have changed us; I can see that our faces are no
nger familiar to you."

"Have we been driven here to die?" Papa asked.

"That is the plan, but Jemal Pasha, the Turkish
mmander and governor of Syria, is not as hard-
arted as the men of Constantinople. Unfortunately,
e Allies have blocked all ports, and the entire wheat
pply of the Haran region has been requisitioned for
e army. What is more, locusts invaded this region
st summer, attacking everything green and growing,
that even the farmers are without food. Naturally,
e will be fed last."

"The hole we have marched into seems to deepen
d widen with every step," Grandpa said.

"Still, some have escaped, and rumors of American
lief are keeping many alive."

"Are the roads to Baghdad and Damascus closed?"

"With money anything can be arranged. Do you
now the Boyajian family?"

"Only the elder, if you are speaking of the rug
ealer from the Armenian quarter of Afyon."

"Yes, that is the family, God rest his soul. His only

son was here with us—with his family: do yo
remember?"

"It has come back to me. And the old man—whe
did he die?"

"In Konya."

"And the son, you say he has escaped?"

"Just last night. He hired an Arab to take him
Damascus. He was terrified that his daughters wou
be taken by the Turkish gendarmes."

"I thought we had been turned over to the Arabs
Papa asked, alarmed.

"Only on the roads. The Turkish gendarmes ha
been billeted in all the townships. At night they con
into the camps and take what they want. They g
from tent to tent and carry our best-looking wome
into town. None that have been taken have returned

Mama let out a cry. The elder looked at her, ar
the expression on his face became even sadder than
was when he first entered our tent.

"Continue," Papa said.

"Krikor Boyajian has three very attractive teena
daughters. He must have gotten word somehow
the gendarmes because the first night here he gav
each of them boyish haircuts and then dirtied the
faces, to make them as unattractive as possible."

"They were saved then?"

"Yes, but every night the gendarmes came, as I to
you, and took more and more of our possessions."

"How long have you been here?"

"Five days."

"And the rains?"

"They began the second night, and it has rained continuously ever since."

"Do you expect the gendarmes tonight?" Mama asked, in an anxious, worried voice.

"Not in this mud. Not anymore. We are prisoners now of the rain, the mud and this new sickness. Our executioner is everchanging, but always death awaits its task."

The days crawled by. We left our tent only to go to the toilet. One day was much like the next. The sickness slowly passed, but everyone was suffering from weariness and fatigue. Finally, one day, it stopped raining long enough for a large fire to be built, and the women cooked pilaf. Once our stomachs were warmed by the hot food our spirits also changed, and everyone began talking about leaving. But that night the rains began again, and for more than two weeks it rained without stopping—letting up now and then for only an hour or two at a time.

One night I dreamed I was swimming . . . the sun was beating down and shooting off the water in electrical sprays of light; I grew tired and rolled over on my back and stared up at the sun—and suddenly I was awake, staring up at the whitish glow the sun's rays were casting on the top of the tent. I was sweating, and I felt warm all over for the first time since we had reached Gatma.

I was alone, but I could hear all the excited voices

just outside the tent. I jumped up and put on m
shoes and ran outside. A fire had been started, an
the women were rolling dough, and the men wer
bringing bundles of sticks from the cluster of bushe
at the edge of camp.

That afternoon we had warm bread, our first h
food since the meal of pilaf we had had two week
before.

Everyone was getting anxious to leave. Mama an
Papa wanted to go to Aleppo, where they had hear
there were refugee camps already set up, and wher
relief was rumored to be on the way. But the elde
who had spoken to Papa the night we arrived sai
that they had been ordered to stay in Gatma unt
further instructions were given. We hadn't seen
gendarme or guard since the heavy rains began.

Slowly, the weather began to clear. All our tim
was spent in looking at the sky and in discussing th
weather. We were dirty and starving, and everyon
was saying that we would die if we didn't leave soor

The following morning I awakened to shouts an
clamoring and the sounds of strange voices.

"The guards have returned!" Papa said. "We mus
hurry and arrange our things; they will be moving u
out."

I jumped up and began putting on my shoes, and a
the same time I told Yeghsa and Apkar what to d
because I could see that they were confused an
frightened. Then I dressed Harutiun and rolled up h

covers. By the time I got the boys and Yeghsa to our wagon most of the tents were already down.

"Yulláh, yulláh, rouah [Get up and go]," the guards were shouting in Arabic, their horses rearing and sliding in the mud, steam pouring out of their nostrils. It was still dark and cold outside.

Papa came hurrying up with our tent folded between his arms, shouting at me to stay with the others in the wagon, while he ran back to help Mama bring the rest of our belongings. Then Grandpa and my uncles came, bringing the tent they had been staying in, along with all their belongings.

Once again we were on the road, moving farther and farther away from Azizya. Mama gave me a small piece of bread to break up and share with the others. After that I fell asleep, and I didn't wake up for a long time.

The heat of the day seemed to have awakened me. We were slowly moving down a long, sloping hill, the land in all directions treeless, yellow, flat.

"Where are we?" I asked.

"In Hell, can't you see!" Grandpa said.

"But how come the guards are still with us? Where are we going?"

"They won't tell us; they say we'll know when we get there," Grandpa said in an angry voice.

"But Papa speaks Arabic; can't he ask them?"

"Shush!" Grandpa said. "You talk too much."

Papa turned and looked at me. "We'll be resting soon. Just as soon as I learn something I'll let you know."

During the rest stop I saw Papa speaking to one of the Arab guards, but all Papa would tell me, once we had started up again, was that we would know tomorrow. "I wouldn't be surprised if the guards themselves do not know," Papa said. "They'll probably only accompany us to a village or station on the road and turn us over to someone else."

"I have heard we are headed for Aleppo," Mama said.

"I don't think so," Papa answered, "we would have turned south on the first road we came to. We know that many have preceded us, and Aleppo is no doubt already choking with its Armenian population."

"What has happened to our lives?" Grandpa suddenly said. "War, revolution, deportations, starvation—and this endless desert, that turns from sand to mud to sand again."

"Remember Grandma," I said, "and Auntie; I pray every night that we'll be going home soon."

Because of the poor condition of the roads, as well as our own weakened condition, we were able to travel only a few miles a day. We were allowed to stop before dark and put up our tents, and if our camp happened to be near a village, as it often was, a young Arab boy would come and sell us kindling for our fires. No doubt he was alerted by the guards, who would always desert us, so they could spend their evenings in the villages. Sometimes the boy who brought the kindling would also have a little food to sell, which was always very expensive because food had become scarce. The evenings were cold, and by now everyone had lice, and the clothes of most of the people were in tatters. All of us were suffering from flea bites, which in many cases resulted in a fever that lasted for several hours. In the early morning the Arab guards—either the ones from the day before or new ones—would ride into our camp, dismount and begin pulling up the pegs of our tents, which would collapse on our sleeping bodies, and then they would start yelling at us to get up and go. Some of the Turkish gendarmes had been almost kind to us by comparison, it seemed. They had often gone about their work in a gentle way, whereas the Arab guards were always harsh and cruel and rough.

One day we came to a crossroad where a group of Turkish soldiers were bivouacked. Our caravan was halted, and we were told to come down from our wagon. Two of the soldiers approached Papa, and after they had exchanged a few words, he followed them into a large tent. We were worried and puzzled, but no one said anything. It wasn't long before Papa emerged from the tent, alone, and walked to where we were sitting.

"What is it, Benyat?" Mama asked.

"I have bad news! The Turkish army is in need of

transportation and supplies, and so they are requisitioning my wagon. I am to take a group of these soldiers to Aleppo, and from there I will be given further orders. I believe I will be going to Baghdad because they showed interest when they learned that I had done business in that city and that I am fluent in Arabic. Their army is desperate for supplies."

None of us was able to speak. Papa and our wagon had been our salvation till now. Although we were speechless, we were all thinking the same thought.

"What will become of us?" Mama asked, holding close to the boys, who were beginning to whimper.

"You will go to Meskene," Papa answered. "It is another two days' journey from here. The settlement there is more permanent than the one in Gatma."

"God never closes every door," Grandpa said in a troubled voice.

"I will return! I will return with food and clothing," Papa said, and turning to Mama, he continued. "You must keep our remaining money carefully hidden, and use it sparingly. I will be able to trade our jewelry and precious stones in the city for food and supplies."

"This war cannot last forever," Uncle Haig said. "Perhaps there will even be work for us in Meskene."

"We will pray!" Mama said, and with that we got up and walked to our wagon. As soon as it was emptied, the soldiers called out to Papa to hurry.

Turning to Uncle Apel, Papa said, "The responsibility for our family now rests on your shoulders, where it will have to remain until I return." He embraced and kissed him, and then he kissed and embraced each of us in turn—and, addressing me, he said, "Be a brave girl, Veron, and one day you and I will go to Baghdad together on a holiday." I smiled and giggled, and all at once everyone was smiling—and then Papa was gone.

The next morning will always be clear in my mind because as we were getting ready to go, Apkar said to Mother, "Put my things together, Mama, I want to carry my pack myself." In her remaining days, Mama would tell this over and over again, to everyone she spoke to; she had become so proud of her eldest son, of his sudden bravery and concern for the family's welfare.

We reached Meskene. It seemed a repetition of Gatma, except that there were many more people. As we approached, the weather began to change, growing dark and cloudy and windy—and it started to rain, and once again we approached our destination in the rain and mud.

It was a much bigger camp than Gatma, and it was just on the other side of town. We were very close to the river Euphrates, which was big and muddy and swollen with the winter rains. By combining our tents, we made a bigger area for us to live in. Uncle Apel went to town the second day to see if he could find some tin and wood, to make our living quarters a little more stable and permanent. Mama asked him to bring some thread, so she could patch our clothes.

Uncle Apel came back in an hour's time, empty-handed, but with a look of relief on his face. "There are no Turkish gendarmes in Meskene," he said, "but we cannot go into town; they say we are sick and will spread our diseases to the townspeople."

"How will we eat then," Mama asked, "if this is to be our permanent stopping place?"

"They said they have women who will come and sell us food."

"And when we no longer have money?" Mama asked, but Uncle only shrugged his shoulders and walked away.

After that, in the mornings, and often at other times of the day as well, Arab women dressed in navy blue robes would come to the tents and sell food. They'd call out, "*Halaab, halaab, lúbin* [yogurt, yogurt, milk]" and "*Khubbus* [bread]." They had put orange peels in their nostrils, so they wouldn't have to smell us.

One morning we heard a familiar voice outside our tent, and before any of us could utter a word, the flap flew open and Uncle Apraham walked in, followed by Barron Varjabed, the boys' teacher in Azizya. We couldn't believe our eyes. It was as if they had come to us from home, and a feeling of joy came over us. When we had calmed down enough to ask Uncle Apraham what had happened, he explained that the Armenian soldiers had been detached from the Turkish army and placed in labor battalions, to work on repairing roads and railroad ties. They had escaped one night, and passing themselves off as Turkish peasants, they were able to find out the destination of the Afyon deportees. They had heard so many terrible stories, and had themselves seen so many horrible sights, that they could scarcely believe we were still alive. Finally, in utter exhaustion, they both fell asleep, with the look of relief and happiness still on their faces.

I used to pray that Papa would return, but Mama said he had gone very far away and wouldn't be back for some time. The weather kept getting colder, and it was always damp, and then the winter rains came in full force. The Euphrates was nearly a mile from camp, but we could hear its roar night and day. More and more people were getting sick. The first to die were the very old and the very young. But no one was grieving anymore.

"*Azatveren? Azatveren?*" the survivors would say about the dying, turning a word of lament into a questioning statement of relief, which meant, "Have they been released, are they free at last?" And even the young boys had to assist in the burials, with from fifty to one hundred people being buried at once in shallow pits. Sometimes a priest would attend these burials, and at other times not. There was no sadness on the part of the mourners, except for the immediate family.

Then the spread of cholera got even worse, until it seemed that the entire camp had become infected. All of us children got sick at about the same time. The boys were the first to get ill; then Yeghsa and I. One day I started vomiting, like the others, and then I was unable to hold my bowels. Harutiun seemed to have gone to sleep, and women were coming in and going out of our tent, and all I could hear were excited whisperings—and then my mother's weeping. I thought I knew what had happened, but I was too weak to move. The next morning Harutiun was gone, and when I looked over at Yeghsa and Apkar, they were both asleep; and Grandpa was missing. My uncles were sick. Mother was busy, and nervous and crying . . . and then I fell asleep. When I awoke, I felt that a long time had passed, and a great quiet had occurred. For a long time I stared up at the top of the tent and tried to come back to myself. When I turned to Mama, only she was there.

Mama hardly spoke anymore.

I would sit by myself and try not to bother her, but I was lonely and sad and afraid. I didn't have responsibilities anymore, and I missed looking after Yeghsa and my little brothers. There was nothing to do, and I couldn't find any girls my age to play with near our tent. I wanted to know how long I had been sick and how Mama had gotten me well, but she didn't want to talk about what had happened to us.

She was gone for long periods of time, but she never told me where she was going or where she had been. One day I followed her. She walked in the direction of the river until she came to a clearing near some stunted trees. It seemed a strange place to go alone because there wasn't anything there. She suddenly stopped walking, and after standing still for a moment, she slowly sat down against one of the trees and began crying. At first only her body shook, and I could hear her sobs, but then she started wailing. I had never heard Mama cry like this before. I was frightened deep, deep inside, and I began running back toward the tents. As I ran, all I could see was a picture of her in my mind as she was at that moment—seated on her legs, her body heaving, lurching away from the tree, and in front of her, three large, evenly spaced stones.

Several of Mama's best friends from Azizya were still with us. We had seldom seen them during our long march, but now they began to visit us in our tent, along with Barron Varjabed, who had always been a close friend of our family. The women liked to hug me and bring me little treats. They cried and said I must be their little girl now, too, but I only wanted my own mama to say nice things to me. I missed her attention, and I wished my papa would come back. I missed Grandma and Auntie and Hrpsime, too, but I tried not to think of the ones who were gone—it was too painful.

I played by myself in front of our tent. I wanted to stay close to Mama, hoping she would soon be herself again.

There was an old man from Afyon in the tent next to ours who sat in front of his tent on a prayer rug, fingering his beads and looking down at the ground. Each day I said hello to him and smiled, hoping he would talk to me, but he'd only mutter, over and over again, "*Hey vakh, hey vakh*, our Armenian nation has blown away; how can we ever be men again and stand on our feet!"

I didn't know exactly what he meant, but I knew I wanted to live; I didn't want to die. I have to see Grandma again, and our house, I thought to myself. I want to go home and have Grandma explain what has happened to us. My wish was very strong, and I was determined that this should happen.

All of a sudden, one morning, we heard Papa's voice calling out to the tea man to bring tea to our tent. He must have known just where we were, because the next thing I knew he was there before my eyes, softly calling my name.

"Papa, Papa, Papa," I cried, and ran and threw myself in his arms.

He kept saying, "Yavroos [dear one]," over and over again, holding me closer and closer.

Mama didn't speak or move. She just sat down where she had been standing, and stared at Papa. "You came too late," she said at last, "they are gone," and then she broke down and started crying.

Papa tried to speak but couldn't. I could feel his body trying to make words. "There are orphans everywhere," he said at last, "I can bring you as many as you like."

"I want *my* children!" Mama sobbed.

We went to Mama together and put our arms around her, and I saw that Papa was crying, too, and then I was crying—but some of my tears were from happiness, because I was united with my mama and papa again at last.

The government had sent Papa to Baghdad for supplies of food and clothing for the soldiers. I heard him tell Mama that he was able to do some trading there and that we had money again. He also brought some food, and we had meat to eat again, for the first time since Adana. But he was unable to stay with us because he had to return to Aleppo with his supplies. He said that he would have to take some of the things he had in his wagon to Damascus, but that as soon as he returned from there, he would come to us again.

The weather had changed: It was dry now, and it felt a little the way it did when it was spring at home, and somehow this gave me hope for the future. Papa returned to us, and this time he didn't go away again. Mama was going to the burial ground every day, and Papa was always going after her and bringing her back. Together we tried to cheer her up, but nothing we did seemed to help. One day she seemed to get worse, and Papa made her lie down. I prayed and prayed, but she wouldn't get up and be the Mama I knew. The women were in our tent all the time now, and they were spending as much time with me as with Mama. I didn't want to go out of the tent anymore, but sometimes I just had to. Then one night I heard Papa get up and leave the tent.

Mama was moaning and tossing from side to side. Papa returned, bringing several women with him, and suddenly there was a great excitement in the tent. All the women seemed to be talking at once. I knew what was happening now, and I heard Mama calling out to me, but the women didn't want me to see her. I was afraid. I didn't want her to die, and I didn't want to see her die, and then one of the women picked me up and carried me to her tent.

In the morning we went back, but Mama was gone, and then I realized that she was dead—my mama was dead. I ran to Papa and clung to him, too frightened even to cry. "Mama's gone, Papa; Mama's gone." I tried to bury myself inside his embrace.

"She still had her red cheeks," one of the women was saying. "It was a broken heart; that's what killed her. She couldn't stand to lose her boys."

"She wasn't even sick," another said.

Papa stayed very close to me. For a long time I didn't think of Grandma or Azizya. I wasn't able to think of anything at all. Papa tried not to let me see his sadness, and he said he wouldn't leave me anymore.

The days came and went. My life was empty, and I felt empty; but every day was a little less sad than the day before, and little by little my hope started to come back. All I remember hearing during this terrible time were the words "Deir el Zor." It was a town in Syria south of us where they were sending all the Armenians to die. That's what Papa said. He said that he had learned that once you went to Deir el Zor, there could be no escape. People were being sent there by the thousands. They were saying that it was the end of the line; the final station; the Armenian graveyard. I knew what death was now, and I knew that the Turk meant to kill as many of us as he could. I don't know why, but I wasn't scared. I felt secure because I had my papa, and I was sure he was going to take care of me.

The rumors concerning our departure for Deir el Zor became stronger and stronger, and the people were becoming more agitated and nervous with each passing day. Finally, we could sense that the time had come. Everyone was talking in whispers because several more guards had come into our camp in the afternoon. That night I was awakened by all the noise and commotion in our tent. Papa was talking to several women and Barron Varjabed. I couldn't make out what they were saying, but I could sense their excitement. Then I saw their belongings arranged in six bundles on the floor behind them. They were the same women who had nursed Mama, her close friends from Azizya.

Papa turned to look at me, but before he could call my name, I jumped up.

"Are we escaping, Papa?" I asked in a loud voice. I had tried to control myself, but I was just too excited. I felt wholly alive again—for the first time since Mama died.

"Shhhh! Quiet, Veron!" Papa ordered. "Quick, get dressed."

One of the women came to me and started to help me get my things together.

"Where are we going?" I asked her in a whisper.

"To Birijik. Your father has bribed one of the gendarmes, but we must be very quiet."

"But where is Birijik?"

"It is three days' journey from here, up the Euphrates River," she answered in her quiet soothing voice. "Birijik is in Turkey, which is again free, at least for now. We are leaving the massacres behind. Once we are there, there will be no more deportations, no more marches, no more suffering."

"But—"

"Shhh, no more questions until we are on the road. Quick! We are almost ready to go."

As we approached Birijik, our road winding along the banks of the Euphrates, we saw great numbers of black birds, flying low across the water and wading in the river's shallows. They had long legs, jet-black plumage and slender necks.

In the distance, high above the opposite bank of the river, we could see a castle on a great bluff that seemed to be rising directly up from the river's edge.

"That's Birijik," Papa said, after we had stared at it for some time.

Soon we were directly across from it, but my attention was distracted by a funny-looking boat, around which a number of people were gathered.

"It's a ferry," one of the ladies said, seeing my interest. "It will be taking us across the river, wagon and all, just as soon as there are enough customers."

It was exciting to drive onto the boat with our wagon. Papa let me sit up front with him so I wouldn't miss anything, but once we were aboard and the horses were tied up, we all got down and went to the front of the boat. There were other people there, some standing, some sitting down. The current was so strong that we were unable to go straight across, and the ferry was pulled downstream in a low arc. By the time we reached the other side we had gone from one end of the town to the other. It was very exciting, but it made me dizzy, and I had to sit down. Then, just when we had nearly reached the other shore, the boat was pulled upstream with heavy ropes, and again, it went back and forth, on a zigzag course. But now we were going so slowly that I was able to stand up and watch what was happening. I found myself looking down at the water, and as we got near the castle, I began to see the pink and yellow walls reflected in broken, shimmering patches on the water's surface—and then I noticed an even black line running beneath the broken colors. It was a moment before I thought to look up at the castle itself, and there, to my amazement, I saw the large black birds again. Halfway up the castle walls, on a long ledge that was part of the rocky wall, these birds had built their bushy nests.

"Papa, Papa, look!" I shouted.

A man sitting near us was smiling at us because of my excitement. "What is the bird called?" Papa asked him.

"Here it is called the Birijikli bird," the man said, "but it is a member of the ibis family and not indigenous."

"It is a migratory bird then," Papa said.

"They come in great flocks every spring, all the way from the Nile Valley, flying up through Palestine and then to Birijik. This is where they stop to nest and summer, before returning home. That ledge is their only home, which is why we call them the Birijikli birds. They have never nested anywhere but on that one wall."

After we had disembarked, Papa drove along the main street, which paralleled the river, on through the bazaar, which he told the ladies to make note of, and then to an inn at the edge of town, where he said he would try to find out where there might be a place for us to live.

The owner of the inn came out to meet our wagon. Papa and Varjabed got down and began talking to him in Turkish. After they had spoken for about five minutes, Papa and Varjabed got into the wagon, and having turned around, we headed back for town. After we had passed the town fountain, we went up a steep street, where young girls with jugs were coming and going for water. It was so good to be in a city again and to listen to the peaceful voices of the people. The next thing I knew, we had stopped in front of a *havloo*, which is a small, walled-in courtyard with a cottage at each corner. Papa told us to wait, while he made inquiries. He was soon back, and we could tell from his smile that he had been successful. Our cottage was a single room, with a dirt floor that had an *ojahk* (fireplace) in the corner. We could hardly believe that it was true. At first no one spoke, and then we all started jabbering at once. We began cleaning up the room and arranging our things. Papa and Varjabed said they would go to town and bring back some food. One of the ladies—by this time I was calling them my *doudous* (the Turkish word for aunties)—began making a fire, and soon we were seated on our prayer rugs, and we began singing one of our church songs—but in low voices, so our Turkish neighbors wouldn't hear us.

After we had eaten, Papa gave us the bad news. He said he was still working for the government and that he would have to leave at once and report to the *kaimakam* in Aleppo. He would take Varjabed with him and find him work, he hoped as his assistant. I felt sad, but I didn't say anything because I knew that Papa had no choice. He *had* to leave.

"You mustn't feel bad, Veron," Papa said, "your aunties are going to take good care of you, and I will come and visit you as often as I can."

I didn't say anything but ran and threw myself into his arms.

"After the war, Veron, we'll all go home. Now, put on your coat. I want to take you to the bakery and present you to the baker so you can have my *tihyn* [soldier's daily bread ration]. Barron Varjabed and I will share his ration, and you will share mine with your aunties, and in this way we will all stay alive."

The bakery was very close to our cottage, so we didn't have to take the wagon. "I want you to learn the way," Papa said.

Papa presented a paper to the baker, and holding my hand, he said, "This is my daughter; my bread ration is to go to her."

"Very well! What is your name, little girl?" the baker asked.

"Veron," I answered, squeezing Papa's hand.

"Very well, Veron, you will receive a loaf of round bread every day. Our bread comes out of the oven in the morning between nine-thirty and ten. You can come any time after that."

I thanked the baker, and Papa also thanked him, and then we left.

My aunties gave me a cloth bag to carry my bread in, so it wouldn't get dirty or fall to the ground. I would carry it back to our house every morning as if I were bringing *maas* (holy bread) home from church. This was my daily chore. After I returned home, I would wait for my aunties to come back from the bazaar so we could eat. They went there every morning to pick up whatever scraps of food they could find: damaged greens that the merchants couldn't sell, as well as spinach or Swiss chard leaves and other vegetable leavings. Using a little flour, they would make a kind of gravy from the vegetable juice, and we would soak our bread in this. Our one small loaf of bread was cut in half, to be divided between the morning and evening meals. We would each get a thin slice at each of the two meals, and we would soak our bread in the gravy and eat our vegetable. No one complained; we were happy to be safe, alive and out of danger.

After we had eaten, I would go off in a corner by myself and play. I talked to myself because I didn't have any friends, making up games and pretending that the rags I had to play with were dolls. My aunties would help me in this, by sewing up some of the rags and stuffing them with others, making them look like dolls and blankets and cushions and other things.

My aunties were very sad and worn out. They went only to the bazaar and back once a day, spending the rest of their time in our home, mending their black clothes and talking to one another in Armenian in whispered tones. All their dear ones were lost or gone, and when I thought about their condition, I realized how lucky I was to have a father to look after me, and a home waiting for me in Azizya. Now that we were safe, I was spending more and more time dreaming about our home and Grandma. I used to pretend that I was playing with Hrpsime and that Auntie and Grandma were in the other room, and we would run in there and complain to them whenever we had a quarrel.

Papa said that he and Barron Varjabed had to go to Baghdad and Basra for the government. He would visit us every few weeks, and he always brought meat when he came. "We need this once in a while," he would say, and smile at all of us. My aunties were happiest when he was there, because he was their protector, too.

Then he would take me by the hand, and we would walk to the bazaar, and he would buy me something nice: a ribbon, or some dried chick-peas and raisins. I always felt safe and secure and important when I was with Papa. I thought that everyone knew what a big papa I had, who traveled and did business all over the world. He wasn't a refugee like us. He would say, "If it wasn't for you, I could have passed myself off as a Turk and gone back to Azizya a long time ago, but I would never leave my little girl behind," and then he would squeeze my hand and smile at me.

We often talked about Grandma. Papa said that he had written her that we would be coming home just as soon as we could. He said the war was still going on, and that we couldn't go home until it was over.

The days would become dull and monotonous again when Papa went away. When I mentioned this to him one day, he said that I shouldn't feel sorry for myself, that instead I should find ways to make my aunties happy. He said that we were all more exhausted from our journey than we knew. I sensed for the first time that he was lonely and worn out. I realized that he had never let me see this before, but somehow I saw it now, while he was speaking to me, and it made me feel very sad for my Papa, and at the same time very grateful for all that he had given me. I thought of all the people who had sacrificed for me. I

ve thanks to God, and I made a promise then and
ere that I would always find ways to make others
ppy, too.

One day Papa said, "Come now, let's take a walk to
e top of the city and get some sun on our faces
nile there is still time."

We sat alone on a large rock for a long time,
joying the silence. The brown and yellow plain on
e other side of the river stretched on forever, and a
w of the large black birds could still be seen, flying
ck and forth.

"Azizya is still our home," Papa said, breaking the
ence, "but the Turk and the Armenian can never be
iends again. I worry about the future. I have one
orry for me and Grandma and Auntie, but I have
other worry for you and Hrpsime and the other
ung ones who have escaped death and must begin
e all over again, with an obliterated past and an
known future. I think a way must be discovered to
found the race in another land, and I believe it
ould be far from here—far from our sufferings and
r scars and our torment, in a world in which our
ns and daughters may be free of our wounds. Try
remember this, Veron, even if it means forgetting
erything else I have ever told you. Try to remember
y words today."

The leaves were beginning to fall from the trees
hen he left, and this was how I remembered his
eparture—the chill in the air, as the sun began to set,
d the swirling leaves under my father's wagon.

It was winter when I saw his wagon again. I was coming home from the bakery, and as I turned the corner, there was Papa's wagon parked in front of our courtyard. I ran as fast as I could, but when I got inside, my aunties were there, and the man seated beside them was not my Papa, but Barron Varjabed. I didn't have to be told why he had come. I stood in the doorway clutching my papa's bread. The aunties called to me, but I wouldn't move. Finally, Barron Varjabed spoke. "He died on his feet, Veron, while we were unloading the wagon. He had no final words."

The next day my aunties told me to go to the bakery for Papa's bread ration.

The baker avoided me until the two women who were there when I arrived had left. He looked at me then and said, "I'm sorry, Veron, it's been stopped. I can't give you bread anymore."

I didn't say anything. Somehow I had expected it, but when I walked to the door and heard him call my name, I felt a sudden shock. At that instant I realized fully what it was going to mean to be without my father's love and support.

The baker came to me, while I stood at the door, frozen, holding on to the latch. "Here," he said, thrusting a loaf of bread at me, "the order came down this morning *after* you got here," and he smiled. I smiled, but all at once I felt I was going to cry. I opened the door and ran.

I didn't know what had happened to Papa's money, or even if he had any when he died. Barron Varjabed said that the government now considered the wagon state property. It wouldn't have occurred to me to ask these questions, but I overheard my aunties talking about it. I didn't say anything. I felt alone in the world, although my aunties said they would look after me and would take me with them when the time came to leave.

Our situation was getting desperate because now we had even less to eat than before. I asked my aunties if there was some way I could earn money or food. I felt able to work, and I would be ten in October, and it seemed to me that I was too old just to daydream and play games anymore.

One day one of my aunties came home with exciting news! She had gotten me a job carrying water for two of our Turkish neighbors. She said that I was to start in the morning, and she pointed out their houses, explaining that I would be using their jugs. She said that one of them was the home of a Hodja (religious teacher), and that I was to pick up the jugs, fill them at the fountain and deliver them to a young Armenian girl who lived by herself in a cottage in their courtyard.

"Who is this Armenian girl?" the other auntie wanted to know. "Is she one of the Hodja's wives, or is she a convert that he has adopted?"

"I don't know," the other auntie replied. "I was unable to ask her. Her name is Narkes."

I had heard that many of the Armenian children and women had converted in order to save their lives

d were living in Turkish homes. I wondered if this
menian girl had escaped death in this way, and I
as very anxious to meet her.

The next morning I fussed over myself, and I kept
stering my aunties, asking them if I looked presen-
ble and if they thought I would be liked. They were
ry patient with me, taking my worries very se-
usly and assuring me over and over that everything
uld go well.

I went to the Hodja's house first. The *hanum* (lady
the house) answered the door and told me to go
ound to the gate in back. The Armenian girl was
iting for me. She was very pretty, with fair skin,
lden-brown hair and large, sad, Armenian eyes. I
ced her at once, and we began talking to one an-
her as if we were old friends. I told her I was from
zizya, and asked her where she was from. All she
id was "Marash," but the way she pronounced the
me of her city made me understand that she had
ffered terribly there. I had been about to tell her all
out Grandma and our garden, but I told her about
y aunties instead. After we had talked for a little
hile, she gave me two clay jugs and asked me if I
lew where the fountain was.

I felt newborn somehow, as I went off to fetch the
ater. This was my first job, and I felt that I belonged
the world in a completely different way.

I was a little frightened of all the people, but most
my fears disappeared once I realized that although
ey were Turks, they were not hostile to me—and

probably didn't even know (or care) that I was Armenian. The hard part of the job was carrying the jug back up the long white steps. I would climb a few steps, stop and rest, then climb a few more. I realized how worn out I was and how badly I needed exercise when I began going up these stairs. I would play games with myself by counting the steps or deciding how many I should climb before I stopped to rest again.

When I finally made it back to the Armenian girl's cottage, she took the water from my hand and, putting her arm around me, took me inside and gave me a glass of water and a piece of halva. We talked for a while, and then she went to their kitchen and came back with a rolled-up flat bread. The ends had been folded in, but I could see it contained something. When she handed it to me, I felt very proud because I had earned something that I would be able to share with my aunties. I tried to peek inside the bread, but I couldn't see anything.

Everyone gathered around me when I got home and we rolled out the bread. Inside was a piece of string cheese and some black olives. We were so happy and excited that we all began talking and laughing at once.

That afternoon I went to the other Turkish family and they were very nice to me, too. They called me by my name, and they were almost as generous as Narkes. They too gave me olives or cheese or halva and once in a while gahvoorma (preserved lamb). The

od was always wrapped in bread, so that it was an
citing surprise to go home and unroll it and see
hat we would have to eat that day.

One day when I went to pick up the water jugs, a
oup of beautiful, well-dressed young women were
:ting around on cushions before a low, round table
aking *sarma* with Swiss chard leaves. They filled a
af, then cut it into small pieces, before placing them
a kettle. All the women wore different colored
ass bracelets, which jingled and sparkled when they
ught the sun, casting colored lights in all directions.
stared at them in fascination. One of them looked
at me and gave a merry laugh. "This is Aleppo-
yle *sarma*," she said, and they all laughed good-
aturedly. "We're going to have a feast to welcome
e new bride."

"When?" I asked innocently, not knowing what
se to say.

"Tomorrow," the lady of the house said, and ad-
ressing the others, she continued. "This is Veron,
ar neighbor, who brings us our water every day."

"May I see the bride?" I asked.

They all laughed again in good humor, their brace-
ts singing and sparkling in the sun. "Of course,
eron," the lady of the house said, "you must surely
me and see the bride, and one day you will be a
eautiful bride yourself."

"Can my aunties come?"

"Surely! Bring them, by all means. It will be a good
xcuse for us to become acquainted."

I ran home and told my aunties, but they said the couldn't go because they had not been formally inv ted, and they didn't have the proper clothes, ar besides, they would be embarrassed because ever one would know they were refugees.

"But I'm a refugee, too," I insisted, growing e cited, because I wanted my aunties to go. "They' having a feast, and we're going to eat Aleppo *sarma*

"What's that?" they all asked, and I had to expla to them how Aleppo *sarma* was made.

The next day Narkes came over because she h. heard that we had been invited, and between us v were able to persuade my aunties to come along.

We no sooner arrived than a shouting began, a nouncing the coming of the bride. We all rushed one side, and suddenly the bride was swept past u so quickly that all I could see was her red veil ar long, beautifully embroidered bridal gown. Ever body started chanting in unison:

> "Mashallah, mashallah
> basha, suer
> eshallah,"

which was a prayer to Allah that the bride rema forever beautiful—and then, immediately followir the last word, they put their hands to their mouth and sent out a ringing tremolo.

It was an even more exciting day than I thought would be. We were all seated at round tables, an soon they began serving us delicious foods: lamb an

ilaf, *sarma* and *koufta* and beans—with pahklava and
nadaeif (honey and walnut pastry) for dessert. I was
so happy my aunties had come. I could see that they
were enjoying themselves, and we would be going
home with warm, full stomachs.

Narkes had become like an older sister to me. She
always took me into her room after I brought the
water, and gave me something to eat before giving me
my bread with the surprise food inside. If the Hodja
and his wife were out, she would take me into the
kitchen and give me something special to eat, and
several times we went upstairs to their living room,
where she opened a chest in which goodies were
stored. She would say, "Well, Veron, which of the
sweets would you like to try today?" There was
kessmeh, candied squares made from grape juice and
cornstarch; *eeda*, a dried fruit of the region that was
golden on the outside and had tiny seeds inside that
were nice and crunchy; dried chick-peas; raisins; *rojig*,
which was similar to *kessmeh*, but had powdered sugar
on the outside and walnuts inside. It was a thrill to
have these treats, especially because I knew Narkes
wasn't allowed to give me anything from the chest.

The time wasn't dragging by anymore. I could
almost feel myself getting older and taller and
stronger. One day I heard my aunties saying that we
had been in Birijik for a whole year.

And then it was summer again—hot, dry and dusty.
One morning Narkes surprised me by asking if I

would like to go with her and the Hodja and his wi
to their summer home. She said it wasn't very f
away, and I wouldn't have to stay if I didn't want t

I told her I would have to ask my aunties.

"If you come, Veron, you won't have to carry wat
anymore. We can work in the garden together ar
learn new songs, and there will be lots of good foc
to eat."

I was tempted, but I couldn't decide for myself if
was a good thing to do. I asked my aunties and the
were happy for me, so I thought maybe it was a goo
thing, and I said I would go.

On the designated day they picked me up wit
their wagon. We left in the morning and arrived b
afternoon. For some reason I watched the road ver
carefully. We made only one turn, which was ju
after we had crossed a bridge by a small, fast-flowin
stream.

It was exciting, at first, to be somewhere new; bu
after a few days I got a little bored, and then I starte
getting restless. I began worrying about my aunties.
suddenly occurred to me that they were having less t
eat now that I was gone. All at once I became ver
fearful—what if they would be gone when I got back
I would be homeless! Where would I go? What woul
I do? I was stacking stones in the garden, and Narke
had gone to the well for some water, when I foun
myself walking away from their house toward th
road. I didn't even bother to go into the house for m

w things. I just hurried as fast as I could down the
ad, fearful that Narkes might see me and call me
ack.

By the time I got to the river I was very thirsty. The
ater was cool and refreshing, and after I had
uenched my thirst, I noticed that I was sitting under
 apricot tree. I reached up and began eating the
nes I could reach, and after I became full, I started
lling my dress, so I could take some home.

When I got there, my aunties were very happy to
e me and to have the apricots I brought them. And
ey had surprising news! Just that morning they had
eceived a letter from Varjabed, who was now living
 Aleppo. He wrote that he was in touch with my
elatives from Afyon. They had survived the mas-
acres and were waiting to go back home. He said
at there would be work for the aunties in Aleppo,
nd that my relatives would take responsibility for
e and, when the time came, take me with them to
fyon and deliver me to my grandmother, with
hom they were in touch.

We were excited and nervous. There was no ques-
ion but that we would go. The next day my aunties
ent to the railroad station, and when they came
ack, they showed me our tickets.

We would be leaving the following day.

We kept saying to one another that it was a new
eginning and that someday soon we would be going
ome. It struck me then that my aunties didn't really

have a home anymore, but I was glad that they wer
feeling happy. They must have relatives somewhere,
reasoned, and they'll be able to make a new life, too.
didn't know that when they delivered me to my
relatives in Aleppo, I would never see them again.

My relatives from Afyon, whom I had never seen before, were my grandfather's cousin, Karnig Dumehjian, his wife, Derouhi, their newly married daughter, Surpouhie, and another daughter, Sonia, who was my age. Their son-in-law, Sarkis, was also living with them, and he and Mr. Dumehjian had opened a coffeehouse in Aleppo to support themselves while they waited for the time when they could return to Afyon.

Like our family, they had been through the massacres, but they had started on their march a few days earlier, and instead of going to Gatma, they had found a way to escape to Aleppo, where their troubles soon came to an end. They had lost a son during the deportations, and I heard them say more than once that if it weren't for the loss of their boy, the deportations for them would have been like a vacation. I suppose that was the way they put it because the sufferings of others, by comparison, had been so

much greater. But whenever they said this, I felt [a]
deep wound within me open, and I couldn't understand how they could be so insensitive to my feeling[s].
I was all alone in the world, but except for the so[n]
they had lost, they were all together—and prosperin[g].
In a way, they were saving my life, and I was gratef[ul]
to them; but I also resented them, and I was enviou[s]
of them—especially of their daughter Sonia. Howeve[r,]
most of the time I was free of these thoughts, becaus[e]
for the first time in years I had enough to eat and [a]
clean and healthy atmosphere to live in.

Aleppo was a new world that was opening befor[e]
my eyes. The wide streets, the handsome white buildings, the beautiful voices that sang out at night fro[m]
the balconies, and the coming and going of horse[-]
drawn carriages over the cobblestones were more lik[e]
a picture of life than life itself. The Arabs of Alepp[o]
looked more like us, and they were not like th[e]
uncivilized Arabs we had encountered in the desert. [It]
was a gay city, and the women seemed very beautifu[l]
to me, with their gold bracelets and tiaras, and thei[r]
high-button shoes that went *ksh-ksh* as they walke[d]
along the paved streets.

One of my jobs was taking lunch to my "uncles,["]
as I called them, at their coffeehouse. I was shown th[e]
way once, and after that I went by myself. I was ver[y]
quick to learn. I would have to hear a song only onc[e,]
for instance, to know the words and melody by hear[t.]
I loved music, and Aleppo was full of song.

On Sundays my uncles would rent a horse an[d]

ggy, and we would ride down Bob-il-Faraj Boule-
rd to the Palace Gardens. This was a thrilling
dventure for me, but it was a joy that was tempered
ith sadness because I felt apart from my relatives,
d this only made me feel more alone than if I had
en left behind by myself.

The schools had opened again for the fall term, but
o one asked me if I wanted to go. They had bought a
w dress for Sonia, and a tablet and other school
pplies for her. I had not liked Sonia before, but
w I hated her. She was spoiled, and I used to think,
e's a fat midget and I'm a skinny little orphan. I
ved school, and I was yearning to learn new things.
didn't want to be behind in my studies when I
turned to Azizya. And so I thought, why *can't* they
nd me, too? They can afford it, and I'm their
lative besides. But I couldn't speak to them about it,
r about my sadness, because I felt they weren't
terested in me.

One day I was preparing water in the laundry room
our courtyard, which we shared with another Ar-
enian family from Afyon. I wasn't old enough to do
e wash, but I would put a powder in the water to
ake it soft, and then, when the wash was done, I'd
ang the clothes on the line and take them down
hen they dried. On this particular day, Madame
arkarian, with whom we shared the courtyard,
alked into the laundry room, and after we had said
ello, and she had watched me work for a few

minutes, she said, "*Vakh, yavroos, vakh,* they're wor
ing you like a maid."

I had heard that Madame Markarian had lost h
parents and two of her three children in the ma
sacres. Although we seldom spoke, she always had
warm smile for me, and there was something in h
voice when she spoke that made me know I cou
trust her. I didn't say anything, but to myself
thought that is just how I feel. She must have unde
stood my sadness, because she continued, "Y
know, my husband is gathering the orphans for t
Reverend Aharon's Orphanage. Would you like
go?"

"Will I be given an education?"

"Of course: Armenian, French, English and gener
subjects are all taught. And you will learn new song
and be with children your own age, who are in t
same situation. But you won't eat as well, or have t
same comforts you have here."

"I want to go! If I can go to school, I want to go!"

"Very good!" she said, smiling. "Come to o
house tonight and speak to my husband. He w
arrange it for you."

That night, after supper, I went through the cour
yard and knocked on their door. Mr. Markaria
answered. He was as warm and kind as his wife, and
liked him at once. He said I should get my thing
together and tell my relatives, and he would come fo
me in the morning.

My relatives were very unhappy when I told them

was going to go to the orphanage. "Aren't you happy here?" they asked.

"Yes, but I want to learn to read and write Armenian."

"We will take you to your grandmother's, and you can go to school in Azizya."

"Yes, but until we go, I want to stay at the orphanage, so I can start my lessons."

"Our friends will say we were not good to you, and that is why you are leaving."

I could see that this was their biggest worry, that people would talk, causing them embarrassment. "No, I like you," I lied. "I will come back and visit you whenever I can."

I was ready for Mr. Markarian when he came for me in the morning. I had put my things into a neat little bundle because he had said that it would be a long walk.

I was frightened and nervous and happy. I felt now that I was doing something with my life, and something was being done for me in return. As we walked along the street, I began to feel a kinship with all the people we saw: the woman shaking her rug from her second-story window; the tea man who smiled at me as we passed him by; the carriage driver and his passengers; the barefoot boys not much older than I, in their long, dirty gray cotton tunics that came down to their feet, their breakfast rolls piled on long, narrow sticks; the peddlers; the shoeshine men; the letter writers—all were involved in the business of getting on with their lives, and so was I.

We turned a corner and came upon an Arab with sweet, smiling face, heading across the street in ou direction. He had on a long tunic that reached to hi ankles, and he was carrying a tray on his head o which were stuck, in rows, scarlet toffee-apples, whil under his right arm he held a three-legged stand. stared at him so intently that I tripped. Fortunately Mr. Markarian was holding my hand, and when h saw what had distracted me, he called to the vendor who graciously and effortlessly lifted the tray off hi head with one hand and placed it on the stand, whic he had opened with the other.

"Pick the one you like, Veron," Mr. Markaria said. "Whenever you think of our walk to the or phanage in the future, you will have a happy associa tion to remember it by."

I had never tasted anything so delicious. I lost al track of time, and I was still licking the stick when heard Mr. Markarian say, "Here it is, Reveren Aharon's Orphanage."

A young girl, with a tablet and schoolbook i her hand, went into the building just ahead of us. Oh I thought, I'm going to be like that girl! I'm going t go to school, too! My wish was coming true, and I fel my arms tingle with happiness and excitement.

We went straight to the office, where an elderl man and a young woman were seated at desks. Mr Markarian exchanged greetings with the man, whe

rned out to be Reverend Aharon, and then, looking
own at me, he said, "Here's another orphan."

"We are happy to have you here with us," Rever-
nd Aharon said, reaching out and putting his arm
round my shoulders.

"She wants to go to school," Mr. Markarian said.
She wants to attend your school so she can learn the
nguage of her people."

"Very good! Very good!" Reverend Aharon looked
t me and smiled. It was a smile of welcome and
oncern. I could see that he was very tired, and very
ld. "What is your name, and how old are you?"

"My name is Veron Dumehjian. I will be ten next
onth."

"I'm going to put you in the middle orphanage," he
aid. "You will be with girls your own age." Then,
rning to the woman at the desk across from his, he
aid, "Get me one of the older girls."

"You're not old enough for this school, and you're
o old for the *mangabardez*. Here the girls have some
hores, but in the middle group you will only have to
o to school. We don't want you to have any respon-
bilities as yet."

When the girl came for me, I thanked everyone
nd said good-bye. She took me to a building that
as on a hill behind the one we were in. As soon as
e got there, I was introduced to the *maireig* (house-
other), a fat woman who was very warm and open
nd friendly. She immediately made me feel at home.
must have been recess time because it was very

noisy and girls were running in and out of the buil-
ing. They seemed so happy to me, and I felt that I ha
come to a place where I would be happy, too—where
belonged. I hadn't had a playmate for a very lor
time, and I smiled at every girl I saw. I hoped the
would like me because I already liked them. The
had what I wanted: school, each other, a housemoth
and a place that was theirs. It hardly seemed possib
that this was going to be my home, too, and that I ha
actually come here to live.

The housemother took me upstairs. We went into
dormitory with made-up mattresses on both sides
the room. "This one will be yours," she said, stoppir
in front of one of the beds; "and that is your close
where you will keep your things. If your clothes a
dirty, you can take them to the laundry room. No
go downstairs and play with the other girls. When th
bell rings, it will be dinnertime, and you can follo
them into the dining hall."

After lunch, Sosi, one of the girls I had played jack
with when I had gone outside, took me to get m
orphanage uniform: a plain blue dress, a blue cap
which had red embroidery trimming on the collar an
pockets, black oxford shoes and black socks. I wa
also given a tablet, a pencil and an Armenian gram
mar book.

"Can I go to school now?" I asked Sosi, after w
had gone upstairs and I had changed into m
uniform.

"Of course! As soon as our break ends, we'll have

124

oreign language lesson, either French or English; hen geography and arithmetic; and then recess. After ecess we study the body, and then we have a singing esson."

"When do we study Armenian?"

"In the morning, after breakfast. Grammar, writing, history, literature—all of the morning is for Armenian. Hey, there's the bell! Let's go!"

Sosi became my best friend, along with Zevart, Vergine, Arpi and Siranoush. We always tried to do everything together. That night Sosi showed me how to make my bed. "We have only fifteen minutes in the morning to wash, dress, comb our hair and make our beds, so you'd better learn now, while there's time."

I couldn't wait to start my Armenian lessons. Lying in my bed that night, after lights had gone out, I was happier than I had been in a very long time.

For breakfast we had a slice of bread, two olives and tea.

"Sometimes we have hot cocoa," Siranoush said from across the table. "It just depends."

"And cheese," Nevart added. "Now and then we have cheese for breakfast, too."

"I don't think I ever had cocoa," I said. "Is it good?"

"Oh, yes, very good!" Sosi said. "For lunch, Veron, we have soup—usually lentil or bean—and a slice of bread."

I could see that the other children were as con
cerned with food as I was, but suddenly the conversa
tion changed to our lessons. Zevart loved to sing, and
she was humming an Armenian song that I hadn'
heard before. She was obviously trying to get i
memorized.

"Did they tell you we sing every Sunday at th
Sabon Khan, Veron?" she said, excitedly.

"You do! No, no one told me. Where is it?"

"Downtown. It is the boys' orphanage. We sing fo
the English officers and the American officers
They're the ones who support our orphanage."

Suddenly the bell rang, and we rushed off to class
My Armenian lessons had finally begun. At first
knew less than everyone else in the class; but
learned very quickly, and in a few months I was one
of the best pupils. Our teacher was very gentle and
patient. She said I was a good learner because I had
quick mind, and because I had a strong desire to
improve myself.

I liked the discipline and order of the orphanage
Everything had to be just so: our beds properly made,
our hair combed and neatly braided; our uniforms
clean and ironed. I liked this. It made me feel cared
for, and it gave my life a direction and purpose. I felt
had a home again, and friends—and I would no longer
be forced to move from place to place.

We went to bed every night at seven o'clock, and
we got up at six o'clock. After supper the housemother read us stories from the Bible. This meant a

reat deal to me because it reminded me of the winter ights at Grandma's when Uncle Apel read from the Bible after supper. I loved God, and I felt that He was ny guide and Saviour. I would pray to Him every ight, thanking Him, always, for the blessings of the lay.

After our Armenian lessons we would have recess. Ve would play hopscotch, or jacks, or a game with a ubber ball; or we would visit with one another, the lifferent groups going off by themselves to talk and augh and gossip. Although I had my special friends, I njoyed visiting with others as well. We were all so lifferent, and this fascinated me. Not only were our ooks different, but our moods and dispositions were lifferent, too.

Sunday morning meant a great deal to me for the ame reason that the Bible stories did, because this vas the day we went to the Sabon Khan and sang in Armenian for "The English," as we called them. Most of our songs were religious, and this brought back ond memories of our church in Azizya. All of us oved going to the Sabon Khan for a number of easons. First of all, it meant going into town, and this vas always thrilling because so much of what we saw vas new to us. Afterward we always had wonderful liscussions about the things we had seen.

When we entered the Sabon Khan, "The English" vould be seated at a long table. We would march in one door and take our places, facing center, and then he boys would come in from another door and stand opposite, facing right. This was the only time we saw the Armenian boys. Although we sang together every Sunday, we were not allowed to meet and talk afterward.

Once we entered the hall, all our snickering and giggling would come to an end, and we would put all our talents and efforts into singing the songs that were meant to show "The English" that we honored their support and were grateful for the opportunity of having a home and a school in which to learn.

Sunday afternoons were often a sad time for me. A few of the girls had visitors, but most of the others went into town, to the camps that had been set up for the refugees, where the remaining members of their families lived. These girls had been placed temporarily in the orphanage so they would receive the kind of care their families couldn't provide, and could continue their schooling as well.

Every now and then, in order to feel that I had a family, too, I would walk into town with some of my friends and visit my relatives. I did it for another reason as well. I wanted to stay in touch because I knew that they would one day take me home to my grandma, and so I felt that I should remain friendly with them. They never visited me. Not once! At first this hurt my feelings, especially since my girlfriends knew I had relatives; but I thought, well, I know what they are, and they proved that they didn't love me when they didn't send me to school with their daughter, so I won't let it bother me, and I'll just pretend I like them, so they don't leave me behind when they eturn home. But most of the time I stayed behind nd played with the girls who were orphans like me. Ve would wait for the girls who had families in town o return, because they always had news, and they lways brought back raisins, or dried chick-peas, or alva, which they would share with us. We always hared what we had because we cared for one an-ther, and loved one another, as if we were sisters.

Once a week we would go to the Turkish bath. Because there were so many of us, the housemother vould have to take a different group every day. Our lay was Tuesday, and it was extra-special because I vould be together with all my friends: Sosi, Zevart, Vergine, Arpi and Siranoush. And we were old nough to bathe ourselves, and it wasn't like the ortures in Azizya, when our families bathed us— lthough the housemother kept a close eye on all of us, to be sure we were good and clean when we left.

At the baths we would stare at the rich and aughty. Arab women, adorned in gold bracelets and iaras, and always wearing white, who would enter vith their attendants. They moved very slowly and leliberately, as if they had all the time in the world. On our way home, we would imitate their walk and gestures. Every now and then we would see one that had a grace that was almost magical, and although we nade fun of them among ourselves, we also secretly admired them, even though we knew that Armenian vomen were not allowed to indulge in this kind of ndolence and sensual pleasure.

We never talked about the massacres. It was as if we
had forgotten about our past troubles, but often they
would surface in different ways. Instead of feeling
blue, we tried to be gay; instead of thinking about
how bad people could be, we strengthened our belief
in goodness. We not only looked after one another,
we spent as much time as we could with the little
orphans in the Mangabardez building. When we had
free time, we would go over there in a group, but I
would also often go by myself. I probably missed my
sister and brothers, but I never looked at it that way. I
felt sorry for the little ones because they seemed so
sad and forsaken.

I'd wander over to the schoolyard where they
played, and if any of them had withdrawn from the
others and looked at all unhappy, I would talk to her,
and try to make her feel better. Or if we went in a
group, we would take a jump rope or jacks with us,

and start games for them, or just sit on the sidelines and cheer them on at their games.

There were new children coming into the orphanage all the time.

Most of the older girls who came to the orphanage in the main building had been taken away or had escaped from Arab homes. In addition to the girls who were forcibly taken or purchased by the Arabs during the deportations, there were many cases where mothers, realizing that they could not feed their children, willingly gave them up to the Arabs. The girls who had been taken were put into harems or became maids, and in some cases they even became brides. Some of them had run away from their Arab homes and had come to the orphanage on their own, but in most cases they had been rescued by the British, who searched the Arab villages and forcibly removed the Armenian girls from their illegal owners. All these girls had been tattooed, either below the lip or on the cheek or forehead. Whenever we saw a new girl with little blue marks on her face, we knew she had been freed from the Arabs. We wouldn't say anything, of course, because these girls felt deeply shamed, and were very unhappy. However, there were cases where Armenian girls had become brides of Arabs, and not all these girls were happy to be rescued. Two of these older girls later escaped from the orphanage and returned to their husbands.

The months rolled by. We were busy with the routine of our lives, and had little time to think about the future, but sometimes I would get together with my friends, especially Sosi and Nevart, and we would talk about what we were going to do after the war ended. With Sosi, who was an orphan, too, I mostly talked about Azizya and my grandma and aunt and cousin. She would become sad whenever she wondered about what would happen to her if the orphanage closed down.

Nevart was from Adana. She had lost her immediate family—her father had been killed in the 1909 massacres, and the others had perished during the long march. Her grandparents had been spared, and she had just recently received a letter from her grandmother, who asked her to return as soon as she was able. This at least gave her hope for the future.

It was autumn. I was now eleven years old. Everyone thought the war would end soon, but if we expressed such hopes to Reverend Aharon, he would always say, "We are Armenians, we do not wait with our hope, we wish with our hope. In this life nothing is certain. Place your faith in God, not in man." But a kind of fever was spreading through the camps in town and at the orphanage as well. We had all grown tired of being refugees, living huddled, frightened, insecure existences. Whatever our fortunes, whatever our futures, we wanted to embark on a new life.

The British gave a special feast on January 6, our Christmas, coming to the orphanage for the occasion. We sang for them in the dining hall, wearing paper smocks specially made for their visit. We had memorized "Silent Night," and we sang it for them as our closing number. They were very pleased, and Reverend Aharon was proud of us. He beamed throughout our performance. We each received a stockingful of fruits and nuts and candy.

It was one of the nicest days we had at the orphanage.

There were indications that we would probably be leaving the orphanage soon. We heard there was a committee that was taking down the names of the youngsters who would like to emigrate to England when the war was over. Sosi got very excited, and for days afterward this was all she talked about. Finally, one day, she announced that she had made up her mind: She would go to England if given the chance. I was happy for Sosi, but I knew what I wanted for myself—to return to Azizya, to my grandmother and aunt and cousin, to our beautiful garden that I spent so much time dreaming about.

Winter passed and spring arrived. We had gone over and over our plans; but still, it was a shock when the war finally came to an end, and it seemed that our dreams were about to be realized at last.

One Sunday, to my great surprise, I was told that I had visitors. I tried to control my excitement because I thought it might be a mistake. "Are you sure?" I said to Siranoush, who had come to fetch me.

"Of course I'm sure; I spoke to them myself."

As we came into the room where the visitors waited, I saw my relatives—the entire clan—sitting by themselves in a corner, looking uncomfortable and out of place. I was proud and pleased and disappointed all at the same time.

They pretended they had missed me, and they said they were pleased to see me looking so well. I wanted to show them around the orphanage, but they said they had an appointment in town and couldn't stay very long. It hadn't occurred to me that they might have come for a reason, but I could tell by the look on Sonia's face that she was about to blurt it out.

"Guess what, guess what?" she said, unable to contain herself any longer.

"*Shhh*," her mother said, turning and touching her husband on the sleeve.

"We are leaving for Afyon on Tuesday, Veron," my uncle said. "By train. Would you like to come home with us today, or shall we come and get you Tuesday morning?"

For an instant I didn't know what to say, because my mind was shooting off in so many directions at once. But then I knew. "Today!" I almost shouted. "I'll get my things—I'll only be a minute." I was suddenly afraid that I would be left behind. I ran upstairs and started to change my clothes—but the clothes I had arrived in no longer fitted me. I was dumbfounded, and looking up, I caught the housemother watching me out of the corner of her eye.

"Oh, *Maireig*," I said, and suddenly burst into

ears. She began walking toward me, and I ran and threw myself in her arms. "I'm going home, *Maireig*! I'm going home!"

She looked down at me and smiled. "You have been one of my joys, Veron. I hope you are returning to a happy home. I'm going to miss you."

"I'll miss you, *Maireig*; I'll never forget you as long as I live."

"Pack your things, and hurry along. You can trade your 'young' dress in for an 'older' dress downstairs."

All my girlfriends were waiting for me when I came down. I rushed over to them, and we all started talking at once, and then we were all crying, and none of us could stop. We promised we would always be friends and never forget one another.

I felt as if I had gained and lost another family.

We were on the train and heading back over the long road I had once traveled with my family. The train I had seen the first day of our march suddenly came to my mind, and it brought back the hurt. I quickly forced the feeling aside by picturing our garden. Grandma was suddenly laughing and calling my name. . . . *My, how you've grown, Veron, come let me look at you; let's go into the garden and pick a melon and sit under your favorite tree . . . the sun has warmed my shoulders, Grandma; I think I'll take off my sweater . . . pretty soon Hrpsime will be home from school; here comes Auntie, she has longed for you so . . . I start running toward her, recognizing her face as we get closer and closer. . . . I hear shouts.* . . . Oh, it was Sonia again, hollering to her mother. . . .

I got up and walked out of the compartment. . . *Look at the mountains, Hrpsime, look at the mountains . . we're going to take a walk, Auntie, we'll be right back.* . . . A voice rang in my ear . . . my eyes focused on the landscape and over the sound of the rattling train I thought I heard a familiar voice . . . yes, and turning, I saw Nevart coming toward me.

"Nevart, it's you!"

"Veron, oh, Veron, this is too good to be true. I thought you might be on this train . . . I'm so nervous . . . let's go where we can talk . . . are you nervous, Veron . . . it's so good to see you. . . ."

We rushed to another compartment and found a place where we could sit side by side. "Are you afraid, Nevart?"

"I don't know, are you?"

"I don't know. . . ."

"Do you miss the orphanage?"

"A little, I guess, but I want to go home. Don't you want to go home?"

"Yes, but I'm afraid. Aren't you afraid?"

"Yes . . . but, oh, Nevart, let's not talk about it. Aren't we lucky we found each other? I was so bored sitting with my relatives."

"Hey, I have some money! Grandma sent me my ticket yesterday, and she included some money. I wanted to come see you, but no one knew where your relatives lived. Let's go see if we can buy some raisins and filberts."

"I'd better tell my relatives where I am, so they don't worry."

All we could find to buy was sugarcane. This made me very happy at first, but as soon as I licked it, I remembered the first time I had had sugarcane, and I was filled with sadness.

"What's wrong, Veron?"

"Nothing. Does everybody in Adana eat sugarcane?"

"Yes, I guess so. I don't know. The children all love it."

"I miss all the things Grandma had in her storage closet. We never had sugarcane, though; we had other things."

"Hey, what's all the shouting about?"

"It's Adana; we're coming to Adana," someone was shouting.

"Oh, Veron, I'm nervous again. Do you think my grandma will recognize me?"

"Of course, she'll recognize you."

"But I've gotten so skinny. . . . Here, take some money, so you can buy *choereg* from the vendors in the station." Forcing some coins into my hand, she jumped up and started running down the corridor.

"You're going home, Nevart," I shouted, running after her, "everything is going to be all right again." She turned, unable to speak, tears running down her cheeks, and then she was gone.

"That's why they call this region Afyon," the conductor said, passing me in the corridor, where I was standing, transfixed, staring out the window at the endless fields of poppies.

"They're all in bloom," I said absentmindedly.

"Yes, you're seeing them at the perfect time. Have you never seen our poppies before?"

I turned to look at him—blinking and trying to focus on his face. It was a moment before I realized that I was crying.

"What's wrong, little girl?" Did I say something wrong?"

"No, it's nothing," I stammered. "I'll be all right, please; I'm sorry; it's not your fault."

He took a step or two backward and then quickly turned and walked away.

I started looking out the window again at the endless rows of poppies, which went on for mile after mile, changing and repeating their colors—white, yellow, orange, pink, red and purple. My feelings kept changing, too, until I no longer knew what I felt, and slowly the waves of colors began to have a soothing effect on me, and I began to feel at peace.

My relatives were wealthy, and their home in Afyon was spacious and comfortable. The morning after our arrival they sent a message to my grandmother, but it wasn't until the following afternoon that she was able to come for me. I wanted to see Afyon; but I didn't want to miss Grandma, and since I didn't know how long it would be before she arrived, I stayed home and waited, expecting her to walk through the door at any moment. I was nervous and anxious and worried, and even a little frightened. All I had dreamed about was returning home, but time and circumstance had not changed in my dreams, and now everything seemed new and different, and I didn't know what to expect.

I was in the living room when I heard the knock on the door. I knew it was Grandma. Surpouhie went to the door, and they exchanged greetings and introductions. I couldn't seem to rise from the cushions I was seated on. I stared across the room at Grandma. She looked different. I could see that her braided hair had been hennaed. Her face was lined, and her eyes were very sad. As she approached, I managed to struggle to my feet, and shaking and wobbling, I threw myself into her arms and held on tight to keep from sinking to the ground.

"My little baby, my little baby," she said, over and over. "Thank God I have you back."

We sat on the cushions, neither of us able to talk. I put my head on her lap, and she stroked my hair. "You shrank before you grew," she said, after a long silence.

I wondered if I was small for my size, or if there was something strange about me. It had never occurred to me before.

"You'll have plenty to eat from now on."

"I'm home, Grandma; I'm home!"

"Yes, darling, you're home."

I found out later that Varjabed had written to her about Papa, so I was sure he had told her about everything else as well. I was grateful that she knew because it was something I didn't want ever to talk about.

We had lunch with our relatives, and then we went home in the carriage Grandma had come in. As we rode through the countryside, which seemed so familiar now because of our train ride, I went over in my mind the questions I wanted to ask Grandma. I knew that her life had seen many changes, and I wanted to be careful not to mention anything that might make her feel sad. She must have read my thoughts, and I was relieved when she spoke first. "Veron, I want to have a *madagh* [celebration feast] for you when we get home."

"At your house, Grandma? Is that where everyone is living now?"

"No, we lost our old house. We're living in your house now."

"Aunt Lousapere and Hrpsime, and Aunt—"

"Hrpsime and Aunt Lousapere have gone to Smyrna."

"Smyrna! Why Smyrna? I don't understand!"

"When Uncle Apraham died, Lousapere felt they no longer had a place in our family, so she took Apraham's share, and her sewing machine and Oriental rug, and went to Smyrna."

"Have you heard from her?"

"Oh, yes, and you must write to her, too, as soon as possible."

"How is Hrpsime?"

"Aunt Lousapere has placed her in an orphanage, so she can continue her education. Aunt Lousapere sews for a living, but she can't make enough money to send Hrpsime to a private school."

It seemed to me that life had been almost as difficult for the ones left behind as for those who had had to leave.

"We're sharing the house with Aunt Arousiag and Uncle Hagop. . . ."

"Uncle Hagop is back?"

"Yes, he has returned, but he's not well. He was wounded in the face."

I felt sad and a little sick. I felt sorry for Uncle Hagop, but I also felt sorry for myself. The one uncle I didn't care for had survived, and my favorite aunt had moved away. I wondered what life was going to be like now in our old home. I had spent so much time dreaming about the old days, but now, suddenly, I was afraid. We were in Azizya now, and as I looked out at the passing streets, I couldn't help comparing them to Aleppo, and by comparison everything seemed shabby and dirty. Had it looked this way when I lived here? I wondered. It seemed so backward now, and the people were mean-looking and forlorn.

"It's the war," I heard Grandma saying. "Every crack and corner of civilized life has been sullied by the stupidity of man."

We had come to our house. I got down from the carriage with my little bundle, which suddenly seemed very precious to me. I stood there staring at our house and garden, unwilling to move.

"Come inside, I'll fix you something cool to drink," Grandma said, standing in the doorway and waiting for me to follow.

"Go ahead, Grandma. I want to go sit in the garden for a minute."

I walked to the tree that Mama and Yeghsa and I had sat under the day we had our little picnic together. The tree had grown and no longer seemed to be the tree I knew. The garden had been abandoned, and all that was growing in it now were weeds. Everything seemed worn-out and finished. I was sorry I had come back. But where would I have gone? To England, with Sosi? I began to remember something Papa had said the last time we were together,

ut at that moment a bird flew to a branch over my
ead and began singing. "Oh, it's you," I said aloud,
lthough I knew it couldn't understand. "I've been
one a very long time"—but with that it flew away. I
icked myself up and headed for the house. I'm not
oing to be sad, I said to myself, and I'm not going to
et the others see how I feel.

Our house seemed so small inside. It *looked* the
ame, but as if all the rooms had shrunk. It was
urnished with Grandma's things, except for the few
ieces I remembered Papa taking to Grandma's the
lay we left. Mariam came running out to greet me,
ut her little brothers hung back, peeking around the
orner and then pulling back. "Come on out, don't be
ashful," I said, "I bet you don't know who I am."
They came, not speaking, and let me hug and kiss
hem. And then Aunt Arousiag and Uncle Hagop
ame and welcomed me home. Aunt Arousiag
eemed to be happy to see me, and said I looked just
ike my mother now. Uncle Hagop looked very sad.
The wound had made him ugly. The left side of his
ace had collapsed, pulling down his eye. He had very
ittle to say, and his smile was pained and forced.

"I've lost my brothers," he said, and began
obbing.

I realized that on seeing me, he had been reminded
f my father as well as his other brothers.

We all sat down at the table, trying from time to
ime to make conversation. It seemed that our indi-
idual sorrows had separated us, even though we

were members of the same family, and we just didn't know how to be of comfort to one another. I didn't understand at first why we were so changed, because I had always thought that blood was such a strong tie, but as time went on, it became clearer to me that what separated people—or brought them together—was the way they responded to their experiences. In this, it seemed, no two members of our family were alike.

"Tomorrow morning, first thing, I'm going to sew you a new dress," Grandma said, interrupting my thoughts. "And then we are going to go to the school and enroll you. Some of your old classmates have returned, and we are having Sunday services at the church again. How would you like to sing in the choir?"

"Oh, Grandma," I said, "I would love that! I sang at the orphanage in Aleppo. Oh, Grandma, that's the nicest thing you could have said to me." I had never forgotten the church choir, or the church songs—and I remembered the white robes, with the red cross, and I was thrilled at the thought that I could be part of the choir and wear one of those robes.

There was something reassuring in Grandma's voice. She made it seem possible that we would be able to resume our lives again in this old place. I was glad that no one wanted to talk about the past, or at least that they didn't talk about it in front of me, and that preparations were beginning to be made for the future.

The next afternoon we went to the school, and nce we were there I didn't want to leave. It had a mell I liked, and I felt comforted by the voices of the nildren. For the first time since I left the orphanage I lt like running and playing and talking and shout-g. I had a place where I belonged again, where I uld share my feelings with others my age.

On the way home I resumed my friendship with haker Tehbelekian and her cousin Seta, who were oth my age. They had been to a private school in ham, which was near Aleppo, and so, like me, they ad kept up with their Armenian lessons.

"I bet they put you with us," Seta said. "We get a pecial lesson from the boys' teacher every day, be-ause we are advanced."

"I hope so," I answered. It felt good to be home gain with my old schoolmates. I felt a deep satisfac-on that I had chosen to go to the orphange in leppo, because now I was not behind in my studies.

"Hey!" Chaker called back, after we had parted. Tomorrow's Saturday; we're having a special picnic t our place; why don't you come?"

" Oh, Grandma," I called when I got into the house
"I'm so glad you made me a new dress becaus
Chaker Tehbelekian has invited me to a picnic at he
home tomorrow."

"That's very good news, *yavroos*; that is just wha
you need."

"What shall I take? I should take something
shouldn't I?"

"Yes, of course, that's what makes it a picnic. Car
you bake or cook?" Grandma said, smiling.

"Oh, no, Grandma, I've never cooked anything in
my life."

"Well, tomorrow will be your first picnic, and
today you will have your first baking lesson. Wha
would you like to take to the picnic?"

"Pahklava, Grandma, I don't think I've had
pahklava more than once or twice since I left home.'

"That's a hard one, Veron, but pahklava is some-

hing every Armenian girl should know how to make,
and maybe this is a good time to start."

As I got ready for the picnic, I could feel a glow
that was unlike anything I had felt in a very long
time. I could remember having felt this way at times,
long, long ago. I had been happy in Aleppo—with my
friends and my school, but that was somehow different. There we were crowded together, often with too
little to eat, and although we had our housemother, it
was not like having one's own grandmother and
home.

"It's good to feel secure and to have a nest that is
just your own," Grandma had said as she watched me
trying to spread the dough the day before. "This is
what every girl needs and every woman wants. You'll
have to resume your homemaking lessons right away.
There's no time to waste. I was married by the time I
was fifteen."

"I want to go to college, Grandma," I heard myself
say.

"What!" Grandma exclaimed, but I could see that
she held back what she was thinking. "Why?" she
finally asked. "And what would you study?"

"Because I want to go. I want knowledge, the way
Papa had knowledge. I want to understand myself,
and I want to see the world. These things will never
be mine if I just stay in Azizya and get married in a
few years."

"But where would you go?"

147

"I think to Smyrna or Istanbul."

"So far away. . . ."

"I could have gone to England, Grandma. They said the orphans could go to England and get an education, but I wanted to come home and be with you."

Grandma looked at me for a long time before speaking. "You don't *look* grown-up, Veron, but you are. You have your mother's visage, but your father's spirit. You will have your wish. You will come into your father's money when you are fourteen, and you will be old enough then to go to college. I'll send you."

I must not have visited the Tehbelekians' home before the massacres, because neither their house nor the grounds looked familiar. Their garden was very different from ours—they had a huge lawn that was surrounded by flower gardens, and there was a tiny stream winding through the lawn and under a wind-mill, which was the only windmill in Azizya. I was particularly fascinated by the windmill. I had seen them only in drawings, and I hadn't really understood that they existed in real life.

Chaker had invited all the girls in our class. This was the first children's party in Azizya since the return of the Armenians from the massacres. Because it was such a beautiful day, the party was held on the lawn, and when Mrs. Tehbelekian brought out the soft drinks, she said, "This is to celebrate the return

148

f the refugees who are now no longer refugees," and we laughed, happily.

Like me, all the girls were wearing new dresses. We sat near the windmill, on each side of the stream, and because the lawn sloped up from the stream, we were in plain view of one another, and we called and talked to each other, enjoying our raised voices and laughter. I couldn't remember ever feeling so carefree and unrestrained. For the first time since we had left home my thoughts were free of the worries of tomorrow. We laughed and talked and played games and sang popular songs. A great weight had been lifted from my heart.

Slowly, our lives fell into a pattern as we began to learn to live with our sorrows and to make a new life. Grandma didn't seem to be the same person I remembered. It must be her age, I thought, because once, when Grandma could see that I was feeling bad about her sadness, she said, "The young heart, not the old, can heal its ache. It is necessary that you feel good about your life, that you do not feel bad about mine. And I don't want you to feel guilty—about anything. Guilt and regret are the great killers."

"But when I watch you sometimes, Grandma, I feel guilty because I have forgotten many things, and you have not, and I don't feel sad the way you do."

"Later you will remember everything. Now you must try to forget, so your growing body and mind and spirit will not be warped or stunted, but will grow straight and true and strong, like the tree in the yard you like to sit under. Like you, it is young and growing, but I am an old tree now that is bent waiting to return again to the earth from which it came."

Saturdays I would go to the older girls and learn to embroider, and on Sundays we would go to church and I would sing in the choir. I had always loved going to church, but now it was extra-special because I was singing in the choir, and also because I went early, with Grandma. It made me very proud to be with Grandma, because she was the most dignified, highly respected and influential woman in our community. She would sit just inside the door at a table on which there was a dish of candles. On entering, each member of the congregation would take a candle and place a coin in the dish. When the mass was over, Grandma would collect the offering and present it to the trustee after the service, and then we would go home. Just the two of us.

Because Mariam was younger than I, and not yet capable of doing work, I was given all the household chores, and I had to look after Arshalous and Garabed as well. I had to bring the water, set the table, wash dishes, and clean house. I also had to take the children for walks, or if they were outside, I had to go bring them in and find games for them to play. I wanted to go out in the evenings to be with my friends, but Aunt Arousiag always called me in and told me to watch the children. She was bossy and lazy, and I hated her. And I hated the children, too, who were always whining and complaining and getting into trouble.

One day Grandma opened Mother's hope chest, and together we took out all of Mother's fine things and examined them one by one. Grandma held up Mother's blue taffeta dress and said she was going to remake it for me. "You're too young for the pink dress and velvet jacket, but someday they will be yours as well."

I was very happy, and I thought, someday soon I would have my own money and go to college and get away from the bratty children and my mean aunt.

I had written to Aunt Lousapere, giving her our news. Her reply was sad. She said she was all alone now, although she was able to visit Hrpsime on weekends, or have her come home. She said her heart was sore for all the ones that were gone, and for those she was separated from, and she hoped I would be able to visit her one day soon because she knew that she would never return to Azizya.

The longer I stayed in Azizya, the older I got, the less I liked my life. It just wasn't enough to be safe and to be home, because home just wasn't home anymore. Because we no longer trusted the Turks, our lives were now confined to the Armenian quarter. The Turks I knew or spoke to in Azizya all said they were sorry about what had happened. They blamed the government, not the civilian population, which they said was innocent. It was true that many had harbored Armenians and had protested their treatment by the gendarmerie, the *bashi bouzouks* (irregulars) and the Kurdish brigands, but it was impossible now for us to trust the Turks again or to forgive them.

My thirteenth birthday had passed, along with another harsh, bitter winter. I had forgotten how cold it could get in Azizya. Then, almost by a miracle it seemed, the poppies were in bloom, and the sun was again our shining companion.

I was beginning to feel an inner restlessness that I thought at first was caused by the change in seasons, but as the days went by I realized that what I was sensing was something external, a new disturbance in the air. Grandma didn't pay any attention to my complaints at first, but one day she admitted to me, after rumors had begun to circulate at school, that the Turks and Greeks were now quarreling.

"Who is Venizelos?"

"The Greek prime minister."

"But what about him?"

"According to the Treaty of Sèvres, the Greeks have been given Smyrna. That they would be stupid enough to think they could just take it doesn't surprise me, but now they are marching into the interior, ready to fight for it."

"Again?"

Grandma didn't answer; she just looked at me with

that expression that meant, even if one were intelligent enough to understand it, what good would it do?

The rumors seemed to have a force of their own, and day by day they grew stronger and stronger until, finally, one afternoon Turkish soldiers came marching into our neighborhood, knocking on our doors and ordering us out into the street.

"We are evacuating the residents of this quarter," they were shouting. "You will be marched to the Turkish section of town. You will go empty-handed and you will return empty-handed—just as soon as the fighting stops."

Before any of us could utter a word, we found ourselves being marched four abreast down our street and through our quarter. As we passed by our church, we could see the Turkish soldiers rushing inside.

"Grandma," I pleaded, "what is happening; why are we being taken away?"

"The Greeks are in the hills, preparing to attack. The wealthy Turks will be moved to our homes, and the soldiers will hide in the church."

"I don't understand!"

"The Greeks are Christians, like us; they won't bomb our church or the surrounding homes."

The moment I understood what was happening I fell silent, and marched along with the others, none of whom had uttered a word. There seemed to be no way out. Once again we were prisoners.

"Tomorrow, the next day, soon—you will return to

your homes. Do not worry!" the Turkish soldiers were shouting as they moved us along.

We were billeted in one of the wealthy Turkish homes. It was growing dark. I took the children into another room and told them to lie down, until their mother came to put them to bed. At that moment a Turkish woman burst into the house. I recognized her as the woman who had nodded to Grandma on our arrival. Grandma had told us she was a friend from the old days. "Quick, *hanum!*" she shouted. "The Greeks are attacking. We must all rush to the mountains at once, before they reach here."

"Hurry, Veron!" Grandma said. "Go put on the children's shoes."

I ran into the other room and sat the children up and began lacing their shoes. Suddenly I was surrounded by an enveloping flash of light, following by a long, long silence—and then nothing.

must have lost consciousness because the next thing
knew I was lying on the floor, the space around me
dark and smoky and strewn with rubble. The walls
on the three sides I could see had all disappeared,
leveled by what I now realized had been a bomb
blast. I began to hear familiar voices, at first as if in a
dream, but then suddenly very clear and urgent. They
were screaming our names, and an instant later
Grandma was kneeling beside me. Arshalous and
Garabed were out of my reach, lying on their backs as
if asleep, and my first thought was, why don't they
get up? Aunt Arousiag and Uncle Hagop were bent
over their bodies and were calling their names, over
and over. It was only then that I realized they were
dead. I felt a dullness in my leg, and looking down, I
was horrified to see that I was sitting in a pool of
blood. Grandma helped me up, and by leaning on
her, I was able to walk into the other room, which
was somehow completely intact. Grandma sat me

down and began bathing my wound. As she washed the blood away from my leg, I was shocked to see that a portion of my calf had been blown away. I felt myself passing out, but Grandma quickly put a cold compress on my forehead.

"The bone is intact," she said, to reassure me. "It hasn't been broken. You'll be able to walk. I'll tie a piece of cloth around it now, and when we get home I'll bandage it properly."

Just then we heard two more explosions in rapid succession, followed by shouting and screaming. We could hear the voices of the people who were pouring out into the streets. I felt frightened but clearheaded and alert. The Turkish woman who had warned us to leave before the bomb fell rushed into the house and said, in a hysterical voice, "The Greeks have ordered the Turks to leave, or they threaten to bomb the city until nothing is left. Oh, *hanum*, what am I do to . . . my children!" and with that she ran, sobbing, out the door.

Grandma finished tying a piece of cloth around my leg, and then we walked ouside. Aunt Arousiag and Uncle Hagop stayed behind with their dead children, but Mariam came with us. We began walking toward home amid throngs of people, who were hurrying along and shouting at one another in high-pitched voices. The pain in my leg began to increase, and it wasn't long before I couldn't walk anymore.

"It's cold," Grandma said, feeling my leg, and the next thing I knew two of our Armenian neighbors had picked me up and were carrying me along.

As soon as we got into the house, Grandma washed my leg again, and then she put some sour dough on the wound before bandaging it with a clean cloth. We weren't home more than two hours when the priest suddenly appeared, followed by several Greeks. "I have brought the medics," he said to Grandma. "They are going to treat the wounded. They feel very bad about the bombings."

The doctor took off my bandage and carefully removed the dough. He washed the wound again and applied his own medicines, all the while talking to the priest in Greek.

"He says the dough is not the right medicine for such a wound, and could have done considerable harm," the priest told Grandma. Then he said to me, "He will give you something for the pain, and he hopes that they will be able to return in a day or two and look at it again."

I wasn't able to walk after that, and by the second afternoon the medicine had run out. The pain returned in full force, but that evening the doctor and his aides came again. The doctor examined my wound, applied new medicines and re-dressed it, all the time speaking to Grandma in a mixture of Greek and Turkish. I later learned that he told her to get me to the hospital in Afyon, which was now under Greek control, as soon as possible because otherwise I would get blood poisoning and would almost surely lose my leg. As soon as they left, Grandma went to

the church, and together with the priest arranged fo
a transport to Afyon for all the people who wanted to
escape. The priest had warned us the night the bombs
fell that it would be dangerous to stay in Aziziya
while the fighting was going on, and he had been
urging those who had relatives in Afyon to leave as
soon as they could. A number of people had been
killed, but apparently I was the only one who had a
wound that required hospitalization.

Grandma decided that Aunt Arousiag should accompany me to Afyon, while she and Uncle Hagop
stayed behind to protect the family property. All
further plans would be dependent on the outcome of
the fighting. We left in the middle of the night in
three horse-drawn wagons. This time there were neither tears nor parting words; we were sure we would
all be seeing each other again very soon.

I fell asleep soon after Uncle Hagop placed me in
the wagon. He sat me next to Perouze, the older sister
of one of my playmates at school. She put her arm
around me and told me to sleep on her shoulder. She
could see that I was feeling drowsy and sick. The next
thing I knew I was awakened by the sound of barking
dogs. I sat up with a start, and it was a moment before
I remembered that I was in a wagon. "We're in the
Armenian quarter of Afyon," Perouze said. We had
just made our first of several stops, and I watched the
people scramble down from the wagon and disappear
into the night.

I had started to doze again when I was awakened by the sound of my aunt's voice. "This is the Dumehjian house," she shouted at the driver. "This is where we get off." She took Mariam's hand, and they started to get out of the wagon.

"Auntie, Auntie," I called out, "please, help me down!"

She turned and looked at me without speaking, and I saw a look of hatred come into her face. "You should have died instead of my children," she said, scowling. "They are dead, and now you have become my burden—thanks to your grandmother."

I was so shocked and frightened that I couldn't speak.

"I'll help you," I heard Perouze say. She got down on her knees and hoisted me onto her back, and we managed, with the help of others, to get down from the wagon. All at once the door opened, and Uncle Karnig came rushing out to meet us.

"She must go to the hospital at once," Perouze said to Uncle Karnig. "Do you know the way? Can you take her?"

"Of course! I'll take her at once in my carriage." He took me in his arms and carried me into the house.

I had never been inside a hospital before. When we drove up in Uncle's carriage, a nurse rushed out with a wheelchair. She was very warm and friendly, and I liked her at once. She spoke Turkish with a Greek accent, and I had difficulty understanding her at first.

"She's going to be your nurse," Uncle said. "I think they've been expecting you."

After she had wheeled me upstairs to a very small private room, she helped me change into hospital clothes. "Sleep now," she said, "and when the doctor comes, he'll look at your wound and change your dressing."

It was just turning light, and I watched the colors on the horizon begin to change. Its beauty was spoiled by the flashing lights and the sound of booming cannons.

I must have slept a long time because the bustle and excitement of the hospital day were in full swing when I opened my eyes. The next thing I knew my nurse was back, along with a doctor, who began examining me and asking questions. He spoke Turkish fluently, without the trace of an accent.

"This is a bad wound," he said, "have you much pain?"

"Not when I take my pills."

"Let me see," he said, taking the packet of pills from my hand and putting them in his pocket. "From now on the nurse will give you your pills at regular intervals." After turning and speaking to the nurse for a moment in Greek, he said, "Maria will take good care of you. She says you are a brave and cheerful girl. Did you know that you are the only young lady we have in this hospital?"

"No, I didn't know," I said, blushing.

"All our other patients are Greek soldiers. You

may want to learn to speak Greek; it will give you something to do, and take your mind off your troubles." With that he turned and started to walk out of the room.

"Please, Doctor," I called after him, "how long will it be before I can go home?"

"Home is Azizya, is that right?" he asked.

"Yes, my grandmother lives there."

"It will be a long time before you can walk again. Maybe one year. You are going to have to be very brave and very patient."

One year, I thought, that's too long even to think about. Maybe something will happen. Maybe I'll be able to go home and have Grandma look after me.

But the days dragged on. No one came to visit me. I grew more and more lonely with each passing day, but in a way I was glad my aunt didn't want to visit me, now that I knew how much she hated me. Day after day I waited for Grandma to come and see me, but she never came, and she never wrote. Maria told me that the post office had closed down after the Turks had been driven out, so that the only way letters could be delivered was by special courier. One day, after several weeks had gone by, she told me that the roads had been closed to all civilian travel and that it would be best if I didn't expect a visit from my grandmother until the war was over. I heard myself gasp. I had opened my mouth, but the words I wanted to speak wouldn't come out. When I looked into Maria's eyes, I realized that this was news that she had been keeping from me. She must have felt very sorry for me because just then her eyes began to tear.

"It's not your fault," I said.

She came and put her arms around me, and we both began sobbing. "I'm not a very good nurse," she said, "I cry too easily."

"I don't feel so sad now," I said, after we had both stopped crying, and she had begun wiping the tears from my eyes.

"You're a very brave girl. And remember what I said to you the day you came here: At the end of every bad road, a good road begins. It is always so."

It wasn't just being alone that had made me so sad; it was also the soldiers. I would be awakened at night by their moaning and crying. They were being carried in at all hours of the night, and as the hospital began running out of space, they began placing mats in the corridor outside my room for them to sleep on. They would look in at me, but they were too sad to talk, or even to smile. I sometimes saw one of them take out a photograph of his mother or sweetheart and, holding it in front of him, begin sobbing, uncontrollably. They were always praying and breaking down, or calling out a lament in their own language. All the while the sound of fighting just outside the town could be heard.

A white-haired four-star Greek general used to visit the hospital two or three times a week, to talk to the men and try to cheer them up. He always looked into my room and called out a greeting in either Turkish or Greek. One day, to my surprise, he entered and began talking to me in Turkish. He seemed very kind and gentle—and also very sad, but in a way I couldn't understand. He said that he had learned from the staff that I was an orphan. He told me he and his wife had never had children, and they felt an emptiness in their lives that they had never known how to fill. As he spoke, I remembered Maria telling me that the general was sorry for me and always asked her how I was feeling, when he visited the hospital.

"This is a soldier's hospital," he was saying, "and no place for a young girl. I know you are sad and lonely and afraid. How would you like to be my daughter?" He paused for a moment, but when I didn't answer, he continued, "I can take you with me tomorrow to my sister's home in Smyrna, and just as soon as the adoption is legal, I'll take you home with me to Athens."

My first reaction was surprise, but when I got over that, I thought, I don't want to be a Greek girl! That would be horrible! But I also knew that I wasn't safe in Afyon. My relatives weren't looking after me, and I felt that at any moment the Turks might defeat the Greeks, and that if they did, my life would be in danger again.

"Yes," I said, simply, not knowing what else to say. "Yes, I'll go with you tomorrow."

It felt good at first to be safe and secure again. The general was a good man, and I respected him, although I didn't know how to speak to him, and he didn't know how to speak to me. His sister was fat and jolly, and she seemed to enjoy fussing over me. Her home was very beautiful. It was elegantly furnished, with lace curtains, and all the rooms smelled of cologne.

I felt I should be happy, but I wasn't. I *was* grateful to the general, because I was certain that he had saved my life; but I felt even lonelier and sadder now that I was safe. For the first time, I began thinking about my parents and my sister and brothers. I felt that if I went to Athens with the general and became Greek, I would not only lose my church and my nation and my grandmother, but in a sense I would lose all those who had died, as well. I *had* to remain an Armenian, a Dumehjian, the girl my parents and grandmother had reared.

One morning, a few days after we had arrived in Smyrna, the general told me to get ready because we were going to the Armenian church to have an interview with Archbishop Tourian, whose permission for my adoption was required before we could leave for Athens.

I became very nervous. I had never even seen an archbishop before. I didn't know how I could possibly talk to him, but at the same time I wanted him to know my deepest feelings.

I was so nervous and agitated on the way to the church that I would have given anything to postpone our arrival. I guess I felt that if I had *enough* time, I might be able to figure out how to behave before the archbishop. I almost forgot that my real aim was to find a way out of my present situation. When we pulled up in front of the church, the attendant wheeled me inside, and we were taken to the anteroom of the archbishop's office, where we were to wait until he was ready to see us. There was a stern-faced guard standing at his office door.

"You know," the general said to me, "the archbishop is now the only government the Armenians have. He must make all the rules and decisions for his people."

The guard opened the door and beckoned to us. The first thing I thought, when I saw the archbishop sitting in his high-backed velvet chair, was that he was like an Armenian king, majestic, noble and all-powerful. He came around from his desk to greet us. I kissed his hand, and then we sat facing him. He and the general began speaking in Greek. I was able to understand what they were saying, even though I had to guess at most of the words. The archbishop thanked the general for saving my life, saying that he knew that the hospital could have been bombed at any moment. The general replied that the worst part of war was the suffering that little children had to endure. After the general's request for my adoption had been granted, the archbishop turned to me and began speaking in Armenian.

"Do you want to be this man's daughter?"

"No! I want to remain Armenian. I don't want to be torn away from my church and my nation."

"You understand that this man is correct in every way, and that he has authority. We can't just take you out of his hands. However, if you can run away and come back to us here, we will be responsible for you."

"I'll do it," I answered.

I watched the road very carefully on our way back. We made only three turns, and they were easy to follow, but to be certain, I went over them in my mind until the route became a photograph that I could see merely by closing my eyes. It took one-half hour or more to cover the distance by carriage, so I reasoned that it would take me from one to one and one-half hours to walk from the general's house to the church. I would have to start in the dark and get to the church before the household awoke and came looking for me. That night, for my prayer, I asked Father God to make my leg strong enough to carry me to the church.

I fell asleep in spite of myself soon after I got into bed; but I awoke in a few hours, and I kept my eyes wide open until it seemed to me that it would soon be getting light. I got out of bed, dressed and slipped out the window in my room. My leg didn't hurt very much at first, but after about fifteen minutes I began to feel a warm wetness moving toward my ankle. I knew it was blood, and so I decided not to look at it or even to think about it. Although I was a little worried, I felt strong and determined, and my only fear at the moment was being caught; but fortunately, I didn't see a single person in the streets. Before long I began to feel an unusual sensation in my leg. I reached down and touched my knee and then my shin. My leg was cold. I straightened up—frightened, remembering how stiff and cold my leg had become the night I was wounded. I must walk without stopping, I said to myself, no matter what! I had made my last turn, and I forced myself forward by reaffirming that I was now on the road to the church. I was becoming nauseated, and by now my stocking was soaked with blood, and my shoe made a sickening sound each time I took a step. I kept pushing and pushing myself forward, until suddenly I saw the church, just ahead.

The attendant at the door recognized me from the

day before, but gave a start when he saw my bloody leg. He rushed forward and picked me up and carried me inside. As we walked through the church, I watched the blood drip from my shoe and make a running pattern on the floor. I no longer felt identified with the blood or the pain because I knew that I was saved—and nothing else mattered to me now. Suddenly the archbishop came marching out of his office, in our direction.

"I've run away!"

"I see . . . I see . . . I see," he kept saying, his head moving up and down, his eyes full of compassionate concern. "Now I'm going to send you to the Armenian hospital, where they will cure your wound."

He turned to his orderly and, taking a pad from his hand, quickly wrote a note that he handed to the attendant. "Take her to the hospital at once," he ordered.

"When you are well again," he said, turning to me, "come and see me, so I can arrange to have you transferred to the orphange."

Our carriage wound its way through the streets of Smyrna, which suddenly seemed very beautiful to me, and I began comparing it in my mind to Aleppo. It was very different, but I was reminded of Aleppo because it was the only other city I had seen that seemed to me to belong to the world of books and pictures.

"This is a very beautiful city," I said to the attendant.

"The most beautiful in all of Turkey—and the most advanced and cultured as well."

"Why is that?"

"Because it is in the hands of the Christians—Greeks, Armenians and Europeans. The Turks have very little to say about how the city is run. All the commerce, all the industry and all the culture are ours. That is why the Turks call it Infidel Smyrna."

"But where are the Turks? I mean, where do they live?"

"That cluster of homes on that hill in the distance, that is the Turkish community."

At every corner I could look out and see a large expanse of water. I had never in my life seen anything like it. "Is that the ocean?" I asked.

"It's called the Mediterranean Sea, the most magnificent body of water in all the world."

We had come to a huge building, which had a bubbling fountain in its courtyard.

"Here we are!" the attendant said.

"Is *this* the hospital?"

"It's not *just* a hospital! It also houses a church, an old people's home and an asylum for the insane."

"Is it all just for the Armenians?"

"Yes, it was donated by the Spartalian brothers. You will see their statues inside the entrance."

After I had been admitted and taken upstairs for bandaging, I was wheeled to the room that would be my home for the next ten months. It contained thirty-two beds in all, and the patients were women of all ages; I was the only teenager.

I must have been exhausted, because once I got into bed I slept for nearly two whole days. I don't think I was awake for more than an hour or two at a time during that period. In between waking and sleeping I kept remembering that Aunt Lousapere was in Smyrna, and that Hrpsime was in an orphanage here, and I wondered how I would be able to find them.

On the third day I sat up in my bed for the first time. I felt a change, not only in myself, but in the room as well.

"It's Sunday," the woman in the bed next to mine said. "I don't think you'll be able to sleep today—it's visiting day."

I watched the different people come in and go out of the room. I was fascinated by the styles of clothing the people were wearing and by all the different accents. Suddenly I saw Aunt Lousapere peering in at the door, her eyes moving from bed to bed. I started to wave, and just then her eyes fell on me—but to my surprise her expression didn't change, and her head just kept moving in a circle around the room.

"Auntie! Auntie!" I called out, waving my arms frantically in the air.

My voice wasn't loud enough to reach her above all the chattering in the room, but just as she was about to turn away, she gave one last look, and that's when she saw me waving and calling to her.

She started walking toward me, staring, then squinting, with a serious, puzzled expression on her face. Finally, she was directly in front of me.

"Aunt Lousapere!"

"Oh, Veron, is that you?"

We threw our arms around each other's necks, and we just cried and cried. There was so much to say that for a long time we just couldn't speak. She would wipe her tears, and she would wipe mine, and then she would cry all over again.

"We have been spared, but so many are gone."

"Oh, Auntie, promise me you'll never say that again. I just can't think about it anymore. Tell me how you found me. How did you know I was here?"

"Thursday night I had a dream. . . ."

"That's the night I escaped. . . ."

"Yes, well, Thursday night your mother came to me in my sleep, and she said, 'Lousapere, the apple I was carrying in my pocket fell into the stream—quick, run and grab it before it floats away.' I ran at once and caught it and held it up for your mother to see, and when she saw me holding it, she smiled. So, when I woke up Friday morning, I went to my neighbor, who understands such things better than I do, and she said, 'Apple means soul in dreams,' so then I knew it was you, and that you must be hurt and in danger. My neighbor said, 'Hurry, go to the diocese; if any refugees have arrived, the archbishop will know.' So that's how I found you."

"My mother is still looking after me, isn't she, Aunt Lousapere?"

"Yes, darling, in every way that she can. She was the best friend I had in this life, and I have always loved you like a daughter, and so she came to me

when you were in trouble. You'll never have to wor
again; I'll always be at your side. The archbishop to
me that your wound is very bad, and that you w
probably be here for a long time."

"I don't know, Auntie, I hope not. How
Hrpsime? Can she visit me soon?"

"I'll bring her next Sunday."

"Is she still in the orphanage?"

"For now, yes. Our arrangement is a compromis
and we miss each other; but I must work very ha
for the little money I get—and this way she can go
school."

"Oh, Auntie, I'm so happy you found me. I'
missed you and Hrpsime so much."

"You know, Veron, I still don't recognize you. Yo
are like a new person to me, except that you look ju
like your mother. You were just a child when you le
Azizya."

"I'm thirteen now."

"And so grown-up."

That was my first day of happiness in such a lon
time. . . . I missed Grandma, but not Azizya. I didn
ever want to see Azizya again. I wished I had neve
gone back, so I could have kept the picture that I ha
had of it from childhood. And of course, I wouldn
have had this wound either.

Auntie visited me every Sunday, and she alway
brought me something special to cheer me up—fru
or candy or a book. It was wonderful to see Hrpsim

172

gain, even though we were very different from one another now, but of course this didn't matter because we were still like sisters. We talked about our orphanage experiences for a while, but I could tell that she didn't like being in an orphanage, and she couldn't understand why I thought I had been lucky to have gone to the orphanage in Aleppo.

Soon after I arrived in the hospital, everyone started calling me Little Hero. I was the youngest person in our ward, and I suppose that was the reason—or maybe it was because of my unusual escape. Once I could get up and start walking a little I enjoyed doing favors for those who couldn't get out of their beds. I tried to keep busy in this way because there weren't any grounds to walk on, or places to sit outside, or books to read—and so the days were very long.

I liked all the women in our room. We were like a family, and I could tell that we had all had similar experiences, because no one wanted to talk about the past. Some of the women called me Little Daughter, instead of Little Hero, and so I called them *Maireig*, and I let them fuss over me, because I could see it made them feel good.

Sunday mornings I would go to church, and in the afternoons Auntie would visit me—but the rest of the week dragged on.

My wound had left a very ugly scar, and I felt sick when the bandages came off and I saw it for the first time. It just didn't look healed, but rather like hardened raw meat. The doctor said that had we been in America I would have been given a skin graft, but this was Turkey and wartime.

"Still, you're just as good as new. You'll have to favor it for a few weeks, but after that you can forget it ever happened."

"I'll never forget it happened."

"Maybe not, but you *can* forget to feel sorry for yourself."

"I don't feel sorry for myself," I said, ashamed because I *had* been feeling sorry for myself.

"Well, how would you like to leave the hospital?"

"Oh, Doctor, can I? Can I?"

"I want to have another look at it in one week, and then I think we can let you go."

I walked as fast as I could to my room, so I could share the good news with my hospital family. They were very happy for me, but sad, too, because I was leaving, and they were being left behind. My *maireig* cried, and I cried, too. It seemed that I was always saying good-bye, but with each ending I had nearly always gone to a better place.

Once again I was seated in a carriage. By my side was my favorite nurse, Christina Gundjian, who wanted to see that I was safely delivered to the archbishop.

I kissed the archbishop's hand, and told him I was well now, and thanked him for all his help. "I want to go to the orphanage, as you promised, and resume my education."

"Yes, of course."

"Her nickname in the hospital was Little Hero," Christina said to the archbishop.

"I'm not surprised. It is courage such as hers that has permitted our nation to survive for as long as we have."

He handed Christina a note, and said, "See that our Little Hero gets properly established at the orphanage, and God be with you both."

The first thing I did after I got settled at the orphanage was to go looking for Hrpsime.

"It won't be so bad now that you're here," Hrpsime said, after I had found her and we had gone off by ourselves. "Mother can visit us both, and we can go to church and school together and—"

"Isn't the school here, in the orphanage?"

"Oh, no! We go to the Armenian school in the morning and walk back to the orphanage at night. Everything is close, even Mama's house. There isn't anything you can't walk to. Isn't Smyrna beautiful, Veron?"

"Oh, yes, it's nothing like Azizya or Afyon."

"The people aren't like us, though. They're very snooty and stuck-up, and they think they are better than the people from the country."

"Well, that's okay; we have each other now, and nothing can harm us anymore."

I felt secure and happy again. I no longer missed Grandma the way I used to. I had my aunt now and Hrpsime, and I didn't have the responsibilities I had when I lived in Azizya, and I could concentrate on my studies. It was winter, but unlike Azizya, it was very warm. Hrpsime said it was always like summer in Smyrna, except for two or three months in winter, and even then it wasn't really cold, and it never snowed.

I stopped thinking about the future or the past. Auntie said that I was blessed with a good disposition, and that I was fortunate to have come through the massacres without becoming embittered. "We

176

ve found a good place to live," she would often say,
nd one day we will all be living under one roof
ain, as we did in Azizya." I still hadn't given up my
eam of going to college, though I rarely thought
out it anymore.

One evening, just before supper, Hrpsime came
nning up to me in the schoolyard, frantic, crying
ysterically, with the words pouring out of her mouth
 fast I couldn't make out what she was trying to say.

"Please, Hrpsime, one word at a time. . . ."

"There's a widow here, and, and . . . her name is
ladame Bosdanjian . . . she wants to adopt an older
rl, and she's very rich—"

"Come to the point!"

"Oh, Veron, they're giving you away! She's going
 take you! That's what everyone is saying, and the
usemother said I should come and find you, so I
now it's true."

At first I didn't want to believe it. Then I started to
y. I didn't want to be torn away from the only
mily I had left. It seemed cruel and unfair, and after
nly two months of happiness.

"Oh, Hrpsime, what can I do?"

"Don't worry, Veron, Mama will help you."

"But how? She can't even support you—and if she
kes me . . . oh, they just won't let her, that's all . . .
ey'll say, 'Then take your daughter, too!' "

"I'm going to run home right now and tell Mama.
on't let them take you before I get back."

Hrpsime ran off, while I walked slowly back to th office. I was introduced to Madame Bosdanjian, wh was told she could return for me the following da After she left, the housemother reminded me that th orphanage was very poor, and that they were oblige to let the oldest and newest girls go first. She wa sorry that I felt bad about leaving, but she knew that was going to a good home.

I went to the dormitory and lay down on my bed. wasn't long before Hrpsime came back—with a bi smile on her face that I couldn't believe was mear for me.

"Mama says I should tell you not to worry. She wi find a way to get you back. She'll never, never let yo go. That's what she said."

I tried to feel hopeful, but it was hard. I jus couldn't see any way out.

"Don't be sad, Veron. You've always had goo luck, haven't you?"

"Yes, I suppose so. . . ."

Madame Bosdanjian came the next day and too me to her home in Gostepeh, a suburb just outsid the city. She was dressed all in black, including black veil. Her husband had recently died, and sh seemed very sad, though she tried not to show it i front of me. She lived in a large two-story house which was elegantly and very expensively furnished She had two young boys, but no daughters. In he own way, I suppose, she was trying to be nice to me

ut her boys were spoiled, and they very soon be-
ame my responsibility. I seemed to be always caught
n the same trap—looking after other people's chil-
ren. I couldn't go to school, and Madame Bosdanjian
vas very strict about her house, and she was full of
ules. Everything had to be just so. Hrpsime had been
ight: These people were too high-tone. The very rich
re miserable, I thought, but it's not the kind of
nisery one can feel sorry for. My only hope was that
untie would somehow rescue me; but the days went
y, and after two weeks had elapsed, I began to lose
vhat little hope I had left.

One afternoon, while I was dusting and cleaning, I
appened to look out the window, and there, coming
p the walk, was Aunt Lousapere, dressed in a way I
ad never seen before. It was such a shock that I let
ut a little laugh and ran into the kitchen.

Madame Bosdanjian answered the door, and after
he usual amenities had been exchanged, Aunt
ousapere told her why she had come.

She explained that she was very disappointed that
he had not been informed of the adoption, because
er niece was not an orphan, but the grandchild of
ne of the wealthiest families in Azizya, and that now
hat the roads had been reopened (this, of course, was
. fabrication), her grandmother was coming to
Smyrna to take her home. She had come, she told
Madame Bosdanjian, to take me to her home, on my
grandmother's orders, because she was en route and

would be arriving either tonight or early tomorrow.

Madame Bosdanjian was both understanding and apologetic, assuring my aunt that she was totally unaware of the circumstances. She immediately called me and asked why I hadn't told her about my grandmother, and what a great shame this might have placed on her name. After all due apologies had been made, and cake and coffee had been served, we got up to leave. Madame Bosdanjian insisted that we let her driver take us to town in her carriage.

"Well, Veron," Auntie said, when we were safely alone in her two-room apartment, "it looks as if you'll be living with me from now on."

"Oh, Auntie, I thought you'd never come."

"I had to do it properly, or she might have become suspicious and gone to the authorities—and I had to find extra work, so I could buy these fancy clothes."

At that we both began laughing so hard that tears started running down our cheeks.

I was so happy to be with Auntie that nothing else mattered. There was no more thought of school, nor was there any news from Grandma. Certain things had ended for me, but they were replaced by new events so I didn't feel cheated or upset. On the contrary, I was grateful to be living in freedom with my aunt—and I was grateful to be alive.

It was the Easter season, and Auntie said we just had to do something nice, because it had always been ach an important time for us when we were home.

"What would you like to have more than anything se?" Auntie said one day. "I want you to be happy is Easter."

"A dress," I answered almost at once. "I would just ve to have a dress more than anything else in the orld, because no matter what we do on Easter Day, othing would be nicer than to have an Easter dress ll my own."

"That's what it'll be then."

We went downtown the following Saturday, and egan looking for a material that I liked. Naturally, I icked out something in light blue, because blue was y favorite color, and it was also perfect for Easter. untie suggested a pattern she was certain I would ke. "This is just what all the Smyrna girls your age re wearing," Auntie said, with a smile.

Hrpsime came home from the orphanage early unday morning, so we could have Sunday dinner ogether. When she saw me in my blue dress, she got o excited and upset that Auntie promised to make er one just like it.

"The same color and the same pattern. I just have o have one exactly like it. It's the nicest style I've ver seen, and the color is just perfect."

The next Saturday, Auntie and I went to every abric store in town, but none of the shops had any ght blue material left in stock. "It's the Easter rush," hey told us. "All the pretty young ladies want to vear blue for Easter."

Hrpsime was so disappointed when we told her that after Auntie and I got home, I said that I wanted to give my dress to Hrpsime, and that we could have one made for me in yellow instead. Auntie wouldn't hear of it at first because she knew how much I loved my dress, but before we went to bed, I made her promise that she would give it to Hrpsime.

Auntie was a floor lady in a tobacco plant. Smyrna
as known for its tobacco and its many fruits, es-
ecially figs, which were exported, and grapes, from
hich Turkey's famous wines were made. Auntie
rranged for me to begin work with her right after
aster, and for the first time in my life I was earning
oney. We would go to work together in the morn-
g and walk home together at night. Friday nights we
ould get our pay, which I always turned over to
untie, who took care of all our expenses. I was
eginning to mature, and to discover for myself some
f the joys and pleasures of life. Smyrna was a gay
nd beautiful city, full of various types of people and
any different nationalities. I had never seen Euro-
eans before—except for a few in Aleppo—but they
ere as commonplace in Smyrna as the Armenians,
reeks and Turks.

At night we would sometimes go to the quay and
alk along the water's edge, passing the crowded

cafés from which music was always pouring fort
Sometimes we would stop and have coffee, but it w
a pleasure just to walk up and down the quay becau
that's what everyone did. It was fascinating to look
the different people, and to feel free in this wa
without either expectation or fear. I would say
Auntie, when we got home from work, "Please, le
just have some cheese and olives, so we can go to t
quay," but she would insist that we eat somethin
hot. Once in a while I got my way; but usually v
cooked a warm meal together, and then, by the tin
we did the dishes, it would be late, and we would k
too tired to go out. But every Saturday—and c
Sundays, after we had visited Hrpsime—we would g
to the quay.

The days went by. It wasn't long before I bega
making friends at work, as well as with some of tl
girls who were our neighbors. Together, we would g
to Chai Mahalehfey, which was the street where a
the young people spent their time. I would get a fe
pennies from Auntie, so I could buy pumpkin seed
We would walk along cracking and eating the seed
There were boys there, of course, and we would fli
with them and they would flirt with us. They we
not at all like the boys back home. They knew how
talk to girls. They weren't bashful or backward—an
of course, they hadn't known any real troubles, s
they weren't sad, and they weren't poor. We woul
only talk, or call out teasing remarks as we walke

long, and this was our fun. It was the way we got to know boys our own age.

But our happiness soon came to an end. During the last days of August 1922 daily rumors began spreading that Afyon Karahissar had fallen to the Turks. The defeated Greek armies were retreating in the direction of Smyrna, burning villages in their wake and collecting the remnants of the Christian population as they moved along. On September 1 they began arriving in Smyrna. They came first in freight cars, followed shortly by every possible mode of conveyance—trucks, horses, mules, oxcarts, camels—as well as on foot. It hadn't rained since May, and the dust that had collected on their uniforms and civilian clothes added to their dispirited, defeated appearance, as they straggled toward the sea and the ships they prayed would carry them to safety. By September 5 they were arriving at the rate of thirty thousand a day, mostly on foot, with their children often on their backs, and their draft animals following behind, with whatever household goods they had managed to salvage. They were a pitiful, heart-rending sight, and as I watched them marching toward the quay, where they rested their worn bodies, and laid down their heavy loads, I had no idea that I would be numbered among them before too many days had gone by.

It was at this point that George Horton, the American consul general in Smyrna, asked his government to mediate between the Turks and Greeks, but the

Americans refused. Instead, they sent destroyers t
protect American lives and property. We did no
know this at the time, but the following day th
Greek General Staff and the entire Greek civil admin
istration were packed and ready to flee Smyrna. Th
city was pitched into a hysterical frenzy. That day th
local papers reported that there were two hundre
thousand local Christians, and an equal number o
homeless refugees in Smyrna, all of them fearing th
worst.

On September 8 the Greek High Commission an
nounced that the Greek administration would ceas
to exist at ten o'clock that night. All official busines
came to a halt. A deadly calm pervaded the city. I
was a moonlit night. There were neither looters no
pedestrians in the streets. The Greeks had left.

Everyone was saying, "Kemal is coming! Kemal i
coming!" and we were all wondering what he woul
do when he came. "The choice," Auntie said, "will b
either exile or death."

The Turkish quarter, silent for the three years tha
the Greeks had been in command, was now armed t
the teeth. The men marched through the streets car
rying their scarlet flags marked with the star an
crescent, and pictures of Mustafa Kemal, their na
tionalist leader.

A cry swept through the Armenian quarter that w
should take refuge in the Armenian church in ou
neighborhood. This church, St. Gregory, was within

he compound built by the Spartalian brothers, and vas the church to which I had often gone to pray vhen I was in the hospital. The iron courtyard door, vhich led into the compound, must have been built or an eventuality such as this, because everyone said hat it was impregnable, and that it would take cannon fire to break it down.

No fewer than five thousand of us thronged into he church, the old people's home and insane asylum, our numbers finally spilling over into the courtyard vhere armed young men took defensive positions, in he event of an attack. Only the routine of the hospital went on as before, and we were told that the supply of food and medicine was very limited.

On Saturday, September 16, the Turkish troops began arriving, followed on Sunday by Kemal and his convoy of cars. Even though we had been in hiding since early Saturday morning, news from the outside managed somehow to filter through to us, and we learned that on Sunday night Kemal met with his aides to decide on the disposition of the Armenians. By Monday morning a cordon of Turkish soldiers had surrounded the Armenian quarter. A public crier was sent through the streets instructing the Turkish inhabitants to leave at once. That afternoon a proclamation was issued forbidding anyone to harbor Armenians. The killing of Armenians and Greeks began.

Early in the morning on Monday Turkish soldiers

arrived at the church gate and demanded entry. We had been advised from the start to remain silent, and this we had done, murmuring our prayers and speaking only when necessary in whispers. Each of us had brought a pack containing our valuables, and what food we had on hand, but the food supply was soon exhausted, and after the second day food was sent over to us from the hospital kitchen. Despite our silence, we were sure the Turks knew we had taken refuge in the church. They came at least twice a day, shouting obscenities at our iron door and assuring us that they would butcher us without mercy once they gained entrance. During these moments the young men of Zeitun and Hadjin would stand against the door, intent and determined, their guns and sabers at the ready, in case the door should be broken down.

On Tuesday, when the wind had shifted away from the Moslem quarter, the Turks began setting fire to the Armenian homes. The streets leading into the Armenian quarter were guarded by Turkish soldiers, and no one was permitted to enter while the looting, massacring and destruction were going on. It wasn't long before the Smyrna fire brigade was using all available manpower in an attempt to confine the fires to the Armenian quarter, but even this was hopeless, since the fires were being set faster than they could be put out.

The hospital kitchen and dispensary ran seriously

short of food and medicines. We were equally worried about conditions outside the hospital. We needed to know if anyone was concerned for our safety, and if the ships in the harbor would be willing to rescue us. Aside from being safe from fire—the church was built completely of stone—we had no other assurance of safety. Christina Gundjian—the nurse who had taken me to see the archbishop after my leg had healed—volunteered to go for help. A wave of hope and excitement swept through the church and courtyard when we learned that she had approached Dr. Minasian and his staff with her plan. Because she knew French, they decided to try to pass her off as a Red Cross worker, and red crosses were sewn on her sleeve and cap.

It wasn't until after her return that we were able to fit the fragments of her story into a coherent picture. What had happened was this:

Before she had gone half a block, she was stopped by Turkish soldiers. They were easily convinced that she was a Red Cross worker, and let her pass. She had been instructed by Dr. Minasian to go to the diocese and seek the help of the archbishop, on the theory that he would be able to persuade either the Americans, British or French to come to our rescue, once they learned of our numbers and situation. When she entered the church, the first person she saw was Hovannes, the attendant. He told her that the Greek archbishop, Chrysostomas, had been brutally murdered, and that Archbishop Tourian had escaped. The archbishops, Hovannes said, had sent a wire to the Archbishop of Canterbury, pleading with him to intercede with the British Cabinet to arrange an armistice with Kemal or, at the very least, to provide protection for the Christian minorities. But this wire was never answered. Hovannes said that the diocese was now powerless, and suggested Christina seek help from the foreign consulates. She went first to the French Consulate, where she was coldly refused. She then went to the theater on the quay that the American Consulate had taken over, but the staff were caught up in the evacuation of their own people, and were too busy to talk to her. She was told to go to the YWCA, where meetings of policy were being conducted. It was there, after two anxious days, that her pleadings finally fell on sympathetic ears. She heard that Dr. Post was in the building, arranging for the safe passage of the orphanage children. He had recently come from Istanbul, and his name was known to her, both because of his good work and because he spoke fluent Turkish. She was able to persuade him to her cause, and gathering together a general and four American sailors, including a chauffeur, they drove to the church. When they reached the gate, Christina called out to our guards, giving her name. As the door slowly creaked open, a large group of Turkish *chettes* (irregulars) appeared, as if from nowhere, but Dr. Post hurried forward, and convinced them that they need not fear the inhabitants of the hospital, who were sick and harmless Christians. And that is how we were liberated from our self-imposed prison.

Auntie and I were in the courtyard when Christina called out. We heard the heated exchange between the doctor and the irregulars though their words were lost in the clamor that went up once the gate had been opened.

We hurried past the irregulars in their baggy trousers and crossed bandoliers, arrayed with daggers. They scowled at us as we rushed forward and lined up behind the automobile, which slowly began winding its way toward the quay. For the first few blocks the auto had to stop every few yards while the men rushed forward and pulled the dead bodies off to the side of the street, so the auto could pass. Every time a body was moved the stench would rush to our nostrils—and we were gasping and gagging. All at once I felt Auntie crying beside me.

"What is it, Auntie? Why are you crying?"

"It's the fires! I'm afraid!"

"But why? They're not near us, and besides, we're headed for the quay."

"I was caught in a fire when I was a child. My brother died, and I almost got . . . oh, Veron—" And she was suddenly crying again, hysterically.

I tried to say something to comfort her, but I just didn't know what to say—no one had ever told me about this episode in her life.

"It's the smell," she said, after she had calmed down a bit.

"Yes, I smell it, too. What is it?"

"Burning flesh. They must be burning the people alive in their homes."

"Try not to think about it, Auntie, please . . . try to think of something else."

As we walked along, French and American dignitaries moved up and down our ranks, asking if any of us were their citizens.

"Why are they asking for their citizens?" I called out.

"All the other countries are neutral," one of the Hadjintze men called back.

"But what does that mean?"

"It means they are only saving their own."

The full impact of what he was saying didn't hit me at once. I looked out at all the ships in the harbor. They are there to save their own people, I realized, but not us. "But why are these people rescuing us then?" I shouted.

The Hadjintze man turned this time and looked at

me. "Because they are men of feeling in whom conscience is still alive. They believe they can save us, and they *want* to save us."

By the time we reached the quay and looked back up at the sloping hill we had descended, all we could see were fires, charred ruins and billowing clouds of gray smoke.

The fire seemed to be following the people to the water's edge, where they were huddled now by the thousands. It was difficult for me to believe that I was a part of this, or even that it was really happening.

"It will all go now," I heard someone behind me say, "by nightfall . . ." but his voice was drowned out as we jostled and pushed our way to the sea and to the numerous silent ships that were sitting in the bay, mute and indifferent.

When we reached the quay, our escort sped away, leaving us to distribute our five thousand souls among the twenty or so thousand bodies that were standing or drifting about, or just sitting exhausted on their bundles. As we moved along as best we could, not knowing what we were looking for or where we should stop, I noticed a group of Armenians with patches of red, white and blue cloth sewn to their sleeves. When I questioned them, they said that the *Simpson*, the American ship, was anchored nearby, and they were hoping by this patriotic display to be taken aboard. Auntie made a face, which meant, let's keep moving! We began pushing our way to the point, where the fires seemed less concentrated. We tried to get as close to the sea as possible, to be out of the reach of the soldiers, who were moving through the crowds, robbing the people in broad daylight and dragging the men away. All the while, the people, like ants, were swarming toward the sea, as orphanages and schools disgorged their inhabitants.

The French, American and British ships were not making a move to help, while the Italians were shouting and gesturing to the people nearest them to jump and swim to their small boats. The men kept jumping in the water and swimming toward the boats, in numbers far greater than the boats could possibly hold.

We finally found a place to stop, and after settling our bundles on the ground, we lay on top of them, suddenly exhausted. As the sun began to set, I watched one of the ships steaming out of the harbor. With some effort I was able to read its name and pronounce it aloud.

"What did you say?" Auntie asked.

"*Simpson*," I answered. "The American ship. I wonder what it means?"

Before long we began to feel the heat of the fires that were rapidly moving toward the quay. The residents of the hotels called to us in Turkish and Greek, "How close is the fire? Are we still safe?"

No one seemed able to answer because our attention was suddenly riveted on the Turkish soldiers just up the street, who were blocking all avenues of escape, so that the fleeing victims had no choice but to take the path of the fire. All at once, a throng of men, women and children broke through the blockade. Their bundles and parcels on fire, they struggled to get free. Some of them were able to throw themselves into the sea, while others just died on their feet, but remained upright, supported by the crushing crowd.

"Turn your eyes away, Veron. It's a nightmare!"

But there was nowhere to turn. A raft, crowded with refugees, was attempting to push off from shore, when two Turkish soldiers flung kerosene over them, and the next thing I knew their raft was a blazing torch. "We're burning; we're burning," was all I could hear, as I turned my eyes away.

By night the entire city was ablaze. We were packed, nearly half a million human beings, in an area a mile and one-half long and no more than one hundred feet wide. The buildings were crashing down into their own gutted cavities, the sound mixing with the howling wind and the crack of rifle fire. Men, as well as a few women and children, were swimming out to the huge ships, but except for the Italians, no one would take them aboard. The English ships were pouring boiling water down on the swimmers. We could see the steam as it rained down on their heads. The Americans were lined up on their decks, their movie cameras turning. By now the quay was so crowded that we had to stand, shoulder to shoulder, and it wasn't long before some of our bundles were lost because of the shuffling and pushing.

The Greek soldiers and local Greek police now began throwing themselves into the ocean, preferring drowning to capture by the Turks.

"There's no way out of this," Auntie suddenly said. "Let's throw ourselves into the ocean and die with the others."

I was stunned. I couldn't believe that she had actually spoken those words. "Something will happen—something *always* happens," I said, stumbling over the words. "Whatever is to happen to all these people will happen to us."

"But what hope is there?"

"Don't say that! What if Hrpsime is alive? She will need you ... what will happen to her without you?" Somehow these last words silenced her.

No one slept that night—we were crushed into a mass, frightened, unable to move or think. The Turkish soldiers were wandering through, robbing people, shooting at the swimmers and carrying off the young women and girls. Fortunately, we were very close to the water's edge, and not as easy to reach as those who had come later.

Had the buildings fallen on us we all would have burned to death, or drowned, but by some miracle their facades stood erect throughout the fires, which by morning had finally burned themselves out.

The day was gray with the smoke of the fires, and

the cracking of timber now could not be distinguished from rifle fire. The wailing and screaming of the people had temporarily ceased. It was the morning of another day, but what it would bring nobody knew. Hundreds of bodies were floating, dead, on the water, including the police, in their beautiful uniforms, as well as the charred bodies of those who had been on the raft.

Auntie handed me a biscuit to eat. I took it without asking her where it had come from. My thirst was so much greater than my hunger that for a long moment I just stared at the biscuit, and then I began licking it.

We stood like that for hours; numb, exhausted, confused, waiting against hope for some miracle to occur.

Late that afternoon a cry went out around us that we were being taken to the beer garden at the end of the point. About one thousand of us were herded together—women, children and old men—and marched off to the beer garden which had escaped the fires because it was on the water's edge and segregated from the other buildings. We began walking, slowly, in the direction indicated. We were marched through a double door into a walled courtyard. We had been led by monks, who now stepped aside and stood against the wooden doors and looked at us with compassion, as we filed inside.

The first people inside the compound formed a line

in front of the fountain, where one of the monks filled a cup of water for each of us as we filed past. Once our thirsts were slaked, we found a place to lie down and sleep.

The next day we were given French bread to eat. A large family was given an entire loaf, a small family a half loaf and individuals a single piece. This was our only food. That afternoon we were given blankets. There weren't enough to go around, but a few of the people had managed to save their bundles, so nearly everyone had something to sleep on. We were kept within the confines of the beer garden, safe for the moment, but cut off from all news, and we had no idea what would happen to us next. Each day we prayed for a miracle.

Except for the morning cry of "Bread is here," which spread like fire once a day through the compound, a pall of silence seemed to have descended on us, for we had quickly chewed over and consumed what little rumor and speculation we had had to feed on.

On the seventh day, French or American sailors—I couldn't tell which—came and told us that Venizelos had sent a boat that was waiting for us at the quay.

We were relieved; we had been saved; but we were too tired and dirty and numb to feel anything more than simple relief. We got to our feet, slowly, and formed lines. We followed the sailors out of the compound. Once again the monks stood at the gate, but this time with entirely different expressions on their faces.

The quay was silent, deserted, dead. Except for a few scattered, smoldering fires, and a small band of irregulars on horseback, there was nothing to be seen—or heard. Our ship, a broken-down tanker, was waiting for us. The quay was strewn with rubble. The Turks had taken what they wanted, and had broken and torn and scattered the rejected remains. It was a hideous, frightful sight—a true picture, I felt, of Hell on earth.

Our hearts were heavy, but the knowledge that we were being delivered from this nightmare sent an electric shock of energy up and down our ranks. The irregulars felt this as we marched by them, and looking down at us from their horses, they began jeering and cursing us.

"We're going to come over there, too," they shouted. "We're going to follow you to Greece and kill you there!"

A force other than our own feet seemed to carry us as a single body, past the Turks and onto the decrepit tanker, which groaned under our weight. We set off at once, the boat moving with the greatest effort over the stilled waters. We began staring out at the white and gray facades of the buildings, which were like the skeletons of bodies whose charred innards occasionally exuded puffs of gray smoke.

The sailors began shouting at us to spread our

weight equally over the boat's length, or we would sink. The shouting of these orders, and the resultant redistribution of weight, seemed to be the captain's sole concern. But it soon became our concern as well, when we realized that the possibilities were very good that our boat would, in fact, sink if we did not heed the captain's orders.

After two or three hours we came to the Greek island of Lesbos, where our tanker slowly came to a stop. We sent out a cheer in unison, the first release of our pent-up emotions we had allowed ourselves. Our happiness was short-lived, however, as we were refused entry because the island had already taken in more refugees than it could afford to keep or feed.

The captain cursed and fumed, and the sailors all grumbled under their breaths; but we slowly turned our boat around and set out again, this time in a southerly direction.

The next island we came to was Samos, where once again we were refused. But this time the captain insisted that we be accepted, claiming that his ship was now ruined and would sink before it reached another port.

"These are the filthy, starving and wretched remains of Smyrna. Without your care they will soon be dead," he roared down at the man we took to be their mayor.

The islanders were actually very hospitable and cheerful. They were what are called *arnavood* in Turkish. The men wore white tights and pleated white skirts, black vests and tiny black caps and black tasseled shoes. The women wore long, dark skirts, white blouses, black vests and aprons, with square dainty shawls over their heads.

After a very brief conference on the quay, each family came forward and accepted a family of refugees. Auntie and I were taken by an old couple who lived in a white stucco four-room house that was clean and sparsely furnished. There were pictures on the wall, and looking up at them, I felt that we had reached civilization again, and I could believe for the first time that we had been saved, and that this island of safety and goodwill meant the beginning of a new life for Auntie and me.

"First bathe," they said, "then eat." Their accents were strange to my ear, and I had difficulty making out what they were saying. Auntie didn't know any Greek at all. We told them we were Turkish-Greeks, thinking this would make them treat us better, but they were such a generous, humble and simple couple that I knew, once our own fears had subsided, they would have treated us with the same kindness no matter who we were.

We sat down to our first hot meal, feeling clean, happy and at peace. The food was Greek, a stew of vegetables and ground meat. It seemed to warm not only our bodies, but our spirits and souls as well. We ate our meal in silence, tears of gratitude welling in our eyes. And then we were given our own room to sleep in, with clean bedding, and a pillow for each of us.

The next day we were told that because of the shortage of food, we would have to leave Samos as soon as possible. Auntie and several other women conferred with the mayor, who arranged for a boat to take them to Piraeus, the harbor town next to Athens.

They left early the following morning, returning before nightfall. I waited on the hill, because the sea was so beautiful to look out on. Just as the first clouds turned to pink, their boat came into view. I knew the moment I saw Auntie's face that she had good news.

"Veron—the orphans are saved!"

"Then Hrpsime is all right!"

"Yes, I'm sure of it. All the orphans are in a camp outside Athens, so there wasn't time. . . ."

"Don't worry, Auntie, we'll go find her as soon as we can. We *are* going to go to Athens, aren't we?"

"Yes, we have brought good news about that, too. The Greek government has pledged its support to all the refugees. They are going to care for us until we can get on our feet. Refugee camps are being set up all over Athens."

The next morning a boat came from Piraeus to take us away. It was just large enough to take half of us at a time, and Auntie and I were included in the first group. There was a feeling of lightheartedness as we boarded the boat and set off. I stood at the rail and watched Samos slowly disappear. I felt that I had never seen anything as beautiful as the Mediterranean, or this island, with its whitewashed homes and its friendly, costumed people. I was happy to be out of Turkey, and to be headed for a new life.

When we got to Piraeus, there were several buses waiting to take us to Athens.

"We are going to the Tetarto Gymnasio," the driver said. He turned out to be one of the relief workers who would help us settle in once we arrived. "It's an old college in the center of Athens."

The college was a two-story rectangular building with a large courtyard. There were already about one hundred Armenians there, and with four hundred of us—we had left the nearly one hundred Greeks who had been with us from the beginning, in Piraeus—it was all that the college would hold.

The laundry room was in the courtyard, and the first thing the relief workers did was fumigate our clothes, to prevent the spread of diseases. Our underclothes we washed ourselves by hand.

Once our clothes were clean, we were taken inside and assigned living quarters. Auntie and I were given a space of approximately seven feet by four feet on the first floor, in what was once the hallway directly inside the back door, now permanently locked. The spaces were parceled out according to the sizes of the various families, and we were able to attain some measure of privacy by stringing up rope boundaries, over which we draped blankets and sheets. We were each given a blanket to sleep on at first, and with the money Auntie had sewn in her clothes we were able to buy extra blankets and two pillows, as well as dishes and utensils, and a little food when we were hungry. Using an orange crate, we made a storage space that we covered with our towels. Here we kept our dishes and utensils and other odds and ends that we acquired as time went on. The crate also served as a table. There was a bathroom down the hall where we were able to take sponge baths.

We quickly became acquainted with our immediate neighbors. On one side of us was a family from Mersin, consisting of a mother and two daughters. Vartouhi was my age, and Shnorhig was a couple of years older. Shnorhig's husband had been taken from her in Smyrna. It was the fate of all the men between the ages of seventeen and forty-five. They were separated from their families during the mass boardings, and taken to the interior, where they were conscripted to work on the rebuilding of the country. But few were actually spared for this purpose.

Our other neighbors were two old women, who seemed to speak only to each other. There was also a young boy, a little older than I, who was quartered near us with his mother and sister. His name was Asadour Kaprelian. He introduced himself one day, and he was always looking for excuses to talk to me. This must have been upsetting to Auntie, because one day she said to him, in the presence of his mother, "This is not the time for that!" And that was the last time I saw him, although Vartouhi mentioned one day that she had heard that the Kaprelian family had moved upstairs.

In the beginning we were fed by the Red Cross in an old government building not far away. We walked over there once a day, around eleven o'clock, and they would feed us out of one huge pot, cafeteria style. Sometimes it would be soup or stew, but we also were occasionally given a breakfast food that was made of rice, cocoa and sugar. This dish I especially loved, because I had a sweet tooth, and sweets of any kind had become a luxury in our lives.

Just as soon as we were settled, Auntie began making inquiries about the orphans. She learned that the Armenian General Benevolent Union was headquartered not far from us. Its people told her that all the Smyrna orphans were in the suburb of Goreen Tos. At the first opportunity we took a bus and went to the orphanage, and to our great relief we found Hrpsime's name on the roster. She was immediately sent for, and we had a tearful reunion on the lawn. It turned out that Dr. Post—along with Christina Gundjian—had also saved their orphanage. She laughed when we told her that Christina was Armenian. She had wondered how it was that a Red Cross lady knew our language. The orphans had been put aboard a ship that left before Smyrna was totally destroyed. Auntie was grateful that Hrpsime had been spared the worst of the horrors.

After that the only times I saw Hrpsime were when she came to Athens. I was very busy looking for a job. After two weeks of searching I finally found work at the Old Palace, embroidering material for dresses. We made different colored smocks for the summer season. My job was embroidering flower patterns on the printed areas, using a fishbone stitch. I'd walk to work every morning by myself because I was the only girl from our "college" who had a job there. We had been given a little money by the government when we got to Athens, but we got only the first of these monthly allotments, because they were stopped as soon as I found work.

Auntie was having difficulty finding work because she didn't speak Greek, but we were able to get by on the little I made. After the Red Cross food had stopped, we cooked our own food with the others in the courtyard. I was able to keep one drachma for myself each week, and on Sundays several of us girls would walk to the Acropolis, buying pumpkin seeds on the way, and we would sit and look out on the city and talk about our jobs, and wonder about our futures. More and more I dreamed of going to America, and these feelings were strongest on Sundays, when in the company of other Armenian and Greek girls my age, we would share our dreams and talk about the lives we might live in far-off places. I would wish at such moments that I was a bird and could fly to America. It looked so easy, because as we sat on those broken steps, the eye could see into an endless distance that itself seemed to be a promise of the future. The picture of us streaming out of the church nd filing up behind the car that had led us to the quay kept coming back to me, because at that moment, the darkest of my life, foreign dignitaries had been searching for their citizens and offering them safety. I wanted to belong to a country that cared for its people in that way, and had the power to insure their safety, even in time of war.

My best friend at the "college" was Geulia. She lived with her family on the second floor. She was a chubby, pretty girl, and she was much braver and more open with the boys than I was. We always walked with the others to the Acropolis on Sundays, and every night before going to bed, we would stand outside the "college" door and talk about our lives. I couldn't be like her, but her lightheartedness appealed to me. I imagined I might have been like her if I hadn't suffered. When I was with her, I felt I was in touch with my own past—a past that I could imagine but that I had never had the opportunity to live.

"You should get married, Veron," she said to me one night, out of the clear blue sky.

"Oh, no!" I exclaimed, but without even considering what she was suggesting. Marriage just didn't seem to pertain to me at all. More than anything, I wanted to be a young girl, though I knew that my time for being a young girl had passed. "I wanted to go to college," I said, after a long silence.

"Armenian girls don't go to college."

"Some do!"

"Well, maybe if your family is very rich. But anyhow, you can't go to college now! There are some nice boys from Smyrna here. I know one who was picked up by one of the Italian boats. He's very romantic."

"I don't think so."

That was how our conversation ended. It was time to go to bed, but that night, and every so often after that, I began turning over in my mind what Geulia had said. I was at the age when Armenian girls get married. College was out, I knew that, and Auntie said that the American quotas for immigrants were virtually closed for this part of the world. She mentioned England and France as possibilities, but after what I had seen, and all that I had heard, I knew that I wanted nothing to do with Europe or England.

The work at the Old Palace was seasonal, and after I had been there just one month, it ended. Geulia still hadn't found work, but she heard that a shoe factory and a candy factory were both looking for help. The two factories were across the street from one another, a short distance from where we lived. I wore a new blue cotton dress, which Auntie had made for my fifteenth birthday. It was a warm, sunny autumn day, and as we walked along, we discussed both jobs.

"The pay is better at the shoe factory," Geulia said, "but at the candy factory you can eat as much chocolate as you like." Geulia liked chocolate even more than I did, if that was possible.

"I think I'm going to try the shoe factory," I said. "We can use the extra money."

"You have to be a Greek, or else pass for one, or they won't hire you," Geulia said, hoping to dissuade me.

"I think I'll be able to pass, but I had better think of a name. Anyhow, you speak perfect Greek, Geulia, wouldn't you like the extra pay?"

"No, I'd rather have the chocolates."

We came to the candy factory. I said good-bye to Geulia and went across the street to the shoe factory.

I said as little as possible during the interview, which lasted only a minute or two, and they hired me. The factory had a terrible smell, but I was glad I got the job because I was going to be making much more than I had at the Old Palace.

I had told the interviewer that my name was Maria Nickalaou, and that was the name I signed every Friday night to get my pay voucher.

My Greek was poor when I started, but feigning shyness at first, and listening intently to the conversations of all the Greek girls I worked around, I quickly became fluent. During our lunch hour we would sing popular songs and do folk dances together. I was overjoyed to be able to participate in these activities.

The girls thought of me as a Greek, but I never forgot that I was Armenian. My nation and my religion were the forces that sustained me and, I felt, guided me to safety during my most difficult days.

One day, coming home from work, I saw Auntie talking to a woman in front of the "college" door. There was something about them—their postures, the expressions on their faces—that made me know they were not having an ordinary conversation. Auntie introduced me, and after we made the customary polite exchanges, the woman excused herself and left.

"Who was that, and why was she looking at me in that way?" I asked Auntie as soon as we were alone.

"She is the mother of a boy of marriageable age, and she is looking for a suitable bride. She had made inquiries, and seems to know a great deal about you. I didn't ask her *how* she came to know so much about you—that would have been impolite—but my guess is that she has spoken to Geulia, because they are also from Smyrna. Well, anyhow, what do you think, do you want to get married?"

I didn't know what to say. It wasn't my place to approve, or disapprove. Traditionally, these matters were decided by the parents or guardian, but of course, these were not ordinary times. I found myself blushing, not knowing what to say, or even understanding what it was I was feeling.

"I told her to bring the boy—and if you liked one another, we would see."

I was speechless, but somehow I was secretly pleased. I knew Auntie was modern, but I had no idea she would actually leave such a decision to me. It would have been unheard of at home—that I knew.

"I don't want you to be unhappy," she continued. "You have seen too much already. If he seems like a good boy to you—and if I can see nothing wrong with him—then I think we should announce the engagement. You're fifteen now. I think the time to marry has come."

I didn't know what to say. I didn't even know what

questions I should be asking. Instead, I made an excuse to leave, so I could run off and find Geulia.

Geulia smiled when she saw me, and so I knew—and she knew that I knew—that she had been responsible for the arrangement.

"He's very handsome, Veron—and *very* romantic. He's the boy I told you about."

"Auntie says I can approve. I don't have to marry him if I don't want to."

"Gee, she's really modern, isn't she?"

"Yes, very modern."

"I never would have thought it. She's so shy and sensitive and quiet. . . ."

"Tell me about him." I was suddenly very excited—and interested!

"His name is Takvor. He plays the mandolin, and he's a waiter downtown, and, ah, let's see, he speaks perfect Greek, like me, and he's very handsome."

"And romantic."

"Yes, *very* romantic . . . oh, Veron, you're teasing!" Suddenly we were both giggling, and then making serious faces and trying to act grown-up, and giggling all over again.

"He used to be a tramway conductor on the quay. The girls were always flirting with him. You'll like him, Veron; honestly you will. Don't be afraid!"

But I was; I was terrified! I had no idea what to expect—what to look out for, what to look forward to . . . but, anyhow, if I don't like him, I don't *have* to marry him, I thought.

That Sunday, Takvor and his mother paid their official visit, as prearranged.

"With God's approval," the mother began, after we had been seated on the pillows and mats we tried to pretend were *minders*, "we have come to ask your niece's hand for our son."

This is nerve-racking, I thought to myself. I wish Geulia were here to lend moral support. I'd better look up at the boy, to see if I like him—but if I look at him I'll blush. I wonder what he's thinking; I wonder what he's thinking of *me*.

"How's your work, Veron?" Takvor asked, to my utter amazement.

I blushed. "Good—thank you."

"You have a pretty dress on. Did you make it yourself?"

"No, Auntie made it for my birthday," I said, blushing. "Blue is my favorite color," I said, to fill in the silence.

Auntie left the room and returned in a few minutes with Turkish coffee. In a way it was easier to talk when my hands were occupied, but then I was afraid I might slurp my coffee, so all my attention went into keeping my composure.

"That's all right," Auntie said, after they had left, "you weren't expected to speak."

"Not at all?"

"Not at all!"

"Oh," I sighed, and suddenly relaxed for the first time that evening.

"I liked him! Did you like him?" Auntie asked.

"Yes, very much. He's so romantic—and confident!"

"The mother will come again in a few days—alone! I'm going to give my consent."

When the mother returned on Tuesday, she said, very simply and without changing her expression, "My son approves. Does your niece approve? May we hope for your consent?"

"Yes, we are going to give our consent."

After that the topic was quickly closed, and after Turkish coffee had been drunk, and a polite interval had elapsed, she left.

Five anxious days went by, and then, on Sunday, they returned again. They came bearing a box of candy, and in accepting their gift, we sealed our promise. The atmosphere was now completely changed. We all smiled and openly showed our happiness, and we behaved in a slightly more familiar way with one another.

Auntie made Turkish coffee, and we each had a piece of candy. Nothing was said about the engagement or the wedding. I understood that these matters would have to be discussed privately between Takvor's mother and Aunt Lousapere. I did wonder

216

though why I hadn't been given an engagement ring, and after they left that evening, I asked Auntie about it.

"We just can't have an engagement party in this place, Veron, and besides, she wants it to be a quick, informal engagement because she is in mourning for her husband, who was murdered in Smyrna by the Turks. We have decided to wait one month only, and then we will have the marriage. And as soon as you are married she is going to Patras to be with her other son, because her daughter-in-law is expecting to give birth by the end of November. You will be living with your husband and his grandmother until she returns."

"Does that mean that I can't wear white?"

"I'm afraid not, since she is in mourning, but she'll buy you something nice—something you like. I'm sure she'll try to please you."

After a few days had passed, Takvor came to the "college" one evening and asked Auntie if he could take me to a movie.

"That would be very nice, Takvor," Auntie said, "but you will have to bring her home early."

Takvor waited outside while I got dressed. I put on my blue dress and the new shoes and stockings that Auntie had bought for me a few days before.

"Did you ever go to the movies when you were living in Smyrna, Veron?" Takvor asked as we walked along.

217

"Only once—with Auntie. It was very nice." (I had almost said "thrilling," but I caught myself.) He's so handsome and self-assured, I thought, I hope he does all the talking from now on.

"I bought you a blue ribbon for your hair."

"Oh—oh, how pretty," I said, blushing again. "Should I wear it now?"

"Why not! Here, let me tie it for you."

Then he took my hand, and we started walking again.

We looked at each other and smiled. No boy had ever held my hand before. We're engaged, I told myself; if anyone sees us holding hands, they'll know we're engaged.

The movie was about a large family. I wasn't able to make much sense of the story line. My mind kept racing ahead to the marriage, and at the same time that I was thinking about that, I was trying to sit just so. I wanted to be alert, but not tense—and to be ready, so I could answer him properly when he spoke to me.

Suddenly the screen was full of people and laughter and high-spirited talking, and this large movie family was gathered before a fireplace and everyone was singing.

"That's what we're going to have," Takvor said, turning to me, "a large family."

I blushed. What a bold thing to say, I thought.

After the movie Takvor said he was sorry that we couldn't go for ice cream, as he had planned, but he wanted to keep his promise to Auntie, and get me home early.

"Any day now," Auntie said the following morning, "Takvor's mother will be buying you wedding clothes."

Auntie was right. That same evening Takvor's mother came and asked if I would come to their house on Saturday so we could go shopping together for wedding clothes.

Auntie told me how to get there. They were living near Omonia—where Auntie said we would probably shop—in tents that had been supplied by the Armenian General Benevolent Union. When I got there, Takvor was sitting outside their tent, playing his mandolin. He was playing one of the popular Greek songs that we often sang at work. I started humming it under my breath.

"Sing!" he said. "Aloud!"

"No, I'd better not; your mother is probably waiting for me."

Just then his mother came out of their tent, and Takvor and I had to say good-bye.

We went shopping in Omonia, just as Auntie had thought we would. We went first to a dry goods store, where I picked out a pink material that was made of cotton and silk. Since I couldn't have white, I wanted the next closest thing—and pink, I thought, was also very feminine. Next we went to a shoe store down the street.

"What kind of shoes do you think will go with the dress we'll be making?"

"Patent leather are the style now," I said. "I would love to have a pair of patent leather shoes for the wedding."

After we had bought the shoes, all that was left were the stockings. I picked out a pair of light-colored silk stockings.

"Not those," she said at once, in what seemed to me to be a very stern tone of voice. "I'm in mourning, and so you will have to wear black stockings—so there won't be any talk."

I was shocked and hurt, but I didn't say anything. *I'm* not a widow; why should *I* have to wear black? I thought. Only widows wear black. How could I wear black stockings at my own wedding? Geulia and Vartouhi and Shnorhig will see me—how will I feel then? I took the black pair, and I tried not to let my feelings show on my face, but I was very upset. I'm a young girl, I thought to myself, I want what's stylish— something that's right for *me*—not for *her!*

She walked me home.

Auntie was waiting for us, and as soon as she left and we were alone, I said to Auntie, "I don't like her; I don't like her *at all!*"

"Why, Veron, what's wrong?"

By now I was crying. "She bought me black stockings. I wanted a light color to go with my dress, and she bought me black ones. If I can't have what I want

220

now—for my own wedding—what is it going to be like later on?"

Auntie didn't say anything at first. "I know what it's like to live with a mother-in-law. Your grandmother is a great woman, but she was very hard to please. . . . And you will be living with two women, not one."

The topic was closed, but that night, without saying a word to me, Auntie went to a nearby refugee camp, where a priest lived who was a well-known astrologist. "I have a niece," she told the priest, "and there is a boy who wants to marry her, but I have a bad feeling about it. I wonder if it is the right marriage for her?"

"Where and when was she born, and what do you know about the boy?" the priest asked her. He took down an ancient astrology book, and after studying it for some time, he turned to Auntie and said, "This marriage should not take place. If it does, the girl will have many children, and she will be very poor and very unhappy for the rest of her life."

The next morning Auntie told me that she had decided not to give me in marriage to Takvor.

"You know best, Auntie," I said, feeling deeply relieved.

"Go and find Geulia and tell her about the black stockings. In a matter of hours your words will reach their proper destination. Then, tomorrow, I'll go to

Takvor's mother and say that your grandmother is coming, and that I must therefore rescind my words and turn all my responsibilities over to her." She paused for a moment before continuing. "This is the best way to do it. We don't want their family pride to be injured."

"Yes, Auntie, I'll go at once."

"Poor Grandma," Auntie said, smiling, "we've been giving her a lot of work lately."

222

Vartouhi, our neighbor, my other good friend at the "college," had become engaged to a boy from Adana, and one day, during my own turmoil, she had left for Kokinya to get married. I hadn't even said good-bye. She had been as excited and as busy with her life as I had been with mine, and we had somehow lost track of one another.

I felt both sad and relieved when my engagement was broken—and Shnorhig, Vartouhi's younger sister, was also feeling a little blue because her only sister had gone away from home. And so we began commiserating with each other and spent more time together. Geulia was a little mad at me at first—I suppose she was embarrassed, and disappointed, too, at what had happened—and she didn't come to see me, and so I thought it best to leave her alone for a while.

Sunday came, and I had nothing to do—nor did I *want* to do anything. I was sitting on the steps of the "college" feeling a little sorry for myself, when Shnorhig came running up to ask me if I would like to go to Kokinya with her to visit her sister.

"Where exactly is Kokinya?" I asked.

"In Piraeus. It's the camp where all the Adana refugees are staying. They all have little tin houses to live in. It's kind of nice."

"I'd love to go! Let's stop on the way to the station, so I can get something for Vartouhi."

We stopped at a candy store, and I bought her a box of chocolates. I couldn't wait to see her again, and meet her husband.

Vartouhi was as happy to see us as we were to see her. But she wasn't her usual self. We hardly had a chance to sit down—her husband and mother-in-law were out—before she grabbed her coat and said, "Oh, Veron, there's a family that wants to see us—do you mind?—oh, please, let's hurry, they're waiting!" And suddenly we were rushing off, winding through a maze of little tin houses. What's going on, anyway, I wondered, it's almost as if Vartouhi had known I was coming—and where is she taking me? I don't know anyone from Adana. But before I could say anything, we were there—in the house of strangers!

The room was full of people, all seated, well dressed and quite obviously expecting company, and obviously us. But why?

After several minutes of uneasy silence, a tray was passed around that held separate dishes containing dried chick-peas, raisins, dates and figs. One of the women got up to make Turkish coffee. Various polite exchanges were being made, but I wasn't able to follow any of it very closely—I guess because of my own confused state.

Suddenly there was a loud shuffling outside the door, and an elderly man walked in without bothering to announce himself. He was carrying a rolled-up Oriental prayer rug over his shoulder.

"Hello, *Amou* [Uncle], welcome!" the men shouted.

"What is this?" he said, in a wild, carefree voice. "Some special occasion?"

The lady of the house motioned to him, and after he had walked over to her and bent over, she whispered something in his ear.

"Oh, *harssountzou* [betrothed]," he bellowed, turning and addressing me, "come forward and let me spread this rug under your feet."

I wanted to sink into the ground—but I didn't have to, because I already felt that I had been reduced to the size of a filbert nut. But I couldn't hide my face, which I now knew was beet red. I looked up at Vartouhi, whose eyes said, this donkey has let the cat out of the bag.

I was somehow able to get to my feet. "I have to leave now," I said, "please excuse me." Vartouhi and Shnorhig jumped up and, excusing themselves as well, rushed out the door with me.

"What have you done to me?" I shouted at Vartouhi when we got outside.

"Oh, Veron, I'm so sorry, please forgive me. They're a nice family, really—they just have an eccentric uncle, that's all."

"But you should have told me!"

"I know—but I couldn't. After what you've been through, I just thought you'd say no—and they are good friends of ours—and I just thought, oh, Veron, forgive me. . . ." With that she threw her arms around me, and we both started crying.

"You can tell me all about it when we get home," I said, after we had dried our tears and started walking back.

Luckily, no one was home, and she immediately began telling me the story.

"Well," she began, "they had been asking me if I knew any nice girls from the 'college'—but wait, I'm getting ahead of myself. You see, the old lady has a son in America who is working and saving his money so they can all go there, and when they do, he wants them to bring him a bride. I guess there aren't many Armenian girls over there—I mean where he lives, somewhere near Chicago. It's called Veeskahntzsun, something like that. Anyhow, they had found a girl for him, but she wanted to bring her mother with her, and he wouldn't agree to that, so he asked them to find an orphan girl instead."

"Oh, so that's it!"

"Yes, but I saw his picture. He looks very decent and proper. And he has a kind face. His mother adores him—he's the eldest—and he sends money to them every month—that's how they live. So he must be a good man—and a good provider."

I didn't say anything. Instead, I changed the subject. It was just too much—and too complicated. I didn't want to think about it. I wanted to go to America—but as a mail-order bride! That wouldn't be romantic at all! Yet, if he made good money, he could offer me security and safety, and a real home with proper food. . . .

On Tuesday they came, just as Auntie said they would, although much sooner than she had expected. They came while I was at work, which made me happy, because I don't think I could have faced them again so soon.

"They were here," Auntie said as soon as I walked in. "They brought a teacher to speak for them. It was quite a show. She was very eloquent, very impressive."

"What did you say?" I asked, suddenly excited.

"I wasn't very encouraging. I asked for his picture. They say he is twenty-eight, but he doesn't look twenty-eight—he looks older."

"Is that why you said no?"

"Oh, Veron, America is so far away! We would never see each other again. And what if something were wrong with him? I wouldn't be there to protect you, or help you. What if he drinks or is a gambler?"

"How does he make his living?"

"That's the other thing. We know what the émigrés

do in America. They work in big factories—sometimes they lose an arm, a leg, an eye. The work is very hard, very dangerous. That's what everyone says."

"Oh, Auntie, all I hear are wonderful stories about America."

"I don't know, Veron, I just don't know."

"It's up to you, Auntie, I'm sure you know what's best." I started to walk out, but then I remembered the one question I'd been meaning to ask. "What's his name, Auntie?"

"Melkon—Melkon Kherdian."

"Mmm—I like his name," I said, and walked out—quickly—because I could feel myself beginning to blush.

On Sunday they came again. The mother, the brother-in-law and the schoolteacher, who did most of the talking.

Nothing was said at first, and by the time I had gone out, made Turkish coffee and returned it was already settled. Of course, I couldn't speak, nor did anyone speak to me. It was all very official and proper, and I wasn't included in the negotiations.

"I used your grandmother once again," Auntie said, after they had left. "May she forgive me! I said she was in Salonika—which may well be the truth, since everyone knows by now that the last of the refugees from Anatolia have been deported there—and that we were expecting to be in touch with her

228

very soon. And so I didn't have the authority to make such a decision."

"What did they say?"

"Nothing! What could they say! I don't think we'll be hearing from them again."

We both fell silent. I couldn't tell what I felt at that moment. I had felt secure in Greece, and I was happier than I had been in a long time—now that we were safe from the Turks—but I wanted to find a way to shape my own destiny, so that I wouldn't always be the victim of outside circumstances. But I wasn't allowed to make such decisions—and in truth, I didn't feel that I was qualified to make them—but I couldn't bear to let life just happen to me anymore. I felt troubled and confused, and I knew that sooner or later I would have to make a jump, deliberately, and on my own, or I would again be a victim.

"Veron! Veron!" It was Geulia, running to meet me as I was coming home from work. "Your bad aunt . . . she-she-she's here," she stammered, beside herself with excitement.

"Are you sure?"

"Of course I'm sure! She asked where you live—just a few minutes ago, and after I told her where, I asked her who she was. 'Arousiag Dumehjian'—that's what she said. 'I'm Arousiag Dumehjian, Veron's aunt.'"

Geulia knew my history—we had exchanged life stories soon after we got to know each other.

"What are you going to do, Veron?"

"Nothing! I'll just go inside and see what she wants."

"You will?"

"Sure!"

When I walked into our room, Aunt Arousiag started to walk toward me with a false smile on her face. "Don't touch me," I said, before she had reached me. "What do you want?"

"I've come to take you back. We escaped with the Greeks to Salonika—surely, you've heard! Grandma is still in Turkey, but she will be joining us very soon."

"Oh, so you've come to take me back because Grandma is coming. First you abandon me, and now you come looking for me. I could have forgiven what you said that night, but when you left me in the hospital and never even visited me, I knew you meant those words. You may have fooled Grandma, but you can't fool me. I'm staying right where I am."

"If she doesn't want to go, she doesn't have to," Auntie said, before Aunt Arousiag could reply. "You can't force her to."

"Well!" Aunt Arousiag exclaimed, and muttering under her breath, she picked up her coat and purse and rushed out of the room.

"She had to come," Aunt Lousapere said. "If Grandma sent her, she had no choice but to come—and she may even have thought that you would go with her."

"With or without her, I'll never go back again."

Another autumn had come and gone. In a way, it was a relief not to have anything to worry about or plan for. I knew this quiet period couldn't last. It was enough to work and rest and have Sundays to myself—or to go with Auntie to visit Hrpsime.

After three months of cold weather, March seemed

warm by comparison. The days were usually bright and sunny—and I felt as I always did in spring, hopeful, eager and certain that something new was about to unfold.

One day Shnorhig was waiting for me when I got home from work.

"What is it, Shnorhig?" I said. "You look as if you've got a bird caught in your mouth."

"The Kherdians were here—they just left! They asked that I speak to you. . . ."

"They did? I don't understand."

"I shouldn't have said that. I mean, they wanted to know if your grandmother has returned, because they wanted to talk to her about you."

"What did you say?"

"I said your grandmother never came; only your aunt came, and you didn't go away with her."

"Auntie's not going to like that."

"I'm sorry, Veron—but they were so nice—so sincere—oh, Veron, why don't you give them another chance?"

"It's not up to me, Shnorhig, you know that."

"I know, but Vartouhi is so happy—maybe you'll be happy, too! And they want to take you to America! Just think, Veron—America!"

"Well. . . ." Everyone knew that I wanted to go to America. That it was my big dream.

"They won't come back again, Veron. That's what they told me."

"What else did they say?"

"They said they would have a big engagement party, and buy you a ring, and have your picture taken, and buy you clothes, and . . . ."

"And they told you to tell me that, right?"

"Right!" A big, uncontrollable smile had spread over her face.

"That's all right, Shnorhig; I'm glad you did," I said, and we both started laughing.

"Should I tell them you're still interested?"

"Well, maybe. . . ."

The next day, Saturday, Auntie went to visit Hrpsime. I didn't have work that day, and I could have gone with her; but I felt like being alone.

That evening, when she returned, I could see the minute I looked at her that something was wrong.

"What is it, Auntie; is something the matter?"

"Oh, Veron," she exclaimed, and started crying. It was the first time I had seen her cry since that day in Smyrna, when she had been afraid of the fires. But her tears now were different—and I couldn't imagine what was troubling her.

"It's Hrpsime—the orphanage is sending away all the older children who have a place to go. They told me I had to take Hrpsime home as soon as possible. Oh, Veron, what are we going to do? I haven't any money, and there is barely enough room here for two. . . . How are we going to manage?"

I put my arms around her. I had never known anyone as kind and loving and sensitive as my aunt.

She was always willing to give—to take less, so that Hrpsime and I might have more. To see her like this, in pain, and unable to find a solution to her problem, made me understand just how much she had done for me in the past.

"Auntie, they came again—the Kherdians. Yesterday! They haven't given up. And, well ... I think I should go. I think I should say yes. It will be good for me, because then I can go to America—and it will be good for you, too!"

"Not like this; I don't want you to go in this way! There will always be room for you with me and Hrpsime—you know that! We are one family!"

"I know, Auntie, but I have a good feeling. I know that I will be doing the right thing."

We didn't say anything more after that. Without speaking, she had given her consent—and I felt a deep sense of relief, and a deep sadness, too. My biggest wish was going to come true—but I knew that I would be losing my aunt, whom I loved, and whose love for me was like a mother's.

The Kherdians came the next day, as I knew they would. And this time Auntie gave her consent.

"This is a very happy moment for us," the brother-in-law said, speaking for the family. "We are going to butcher a lamb for the engagement party."

Auntie smiled her approval.

"Veron," Osanna, Melkon's sister, said, "I would like to come on Saturday and take you shopping downtown. And then, on the following Saturday, by which time your new clothes will be ready, we can have the engagement party."

"Yes," I said, simply, suddenly feeling very empty and quiet.

Osanna had come to fetch me from work on the Friday following our shopping day, and together we went to pick up my clothes.

We had chosen a rust-colored wool, which we had the tailor make into a simple, but very stylish, dress. Osanna also bought me a new slip, stockings, shoes and a hand-embroidered purse. I couldn't wait to get home and try everything on.

Auntie looked very pleased when I was all dressed up.

"How do I look, Auntie?"

"Like a young woman; a beautiful young woman—and a lady!"

I had an overwhelming wish at that moment to take Auntie to America with me, but I knew it wasn't possible, so I didn't say anything.

"Tomorrow's the day," I said.

"We must get up early and get ready. Is Geulia coming with us?"

"Of course—and Shnorhig, too!"

When I got up the next morning, I could see from Auntie's eyes that she had been crying.

"I didn't sleep all night, Veron."

"Don't worry, Auntie, please. I told you, I have a

235

good feeling—I know I'm going to have a good life in America."

"I'm sure you will, Veron, but I won't be there—and I don't know if we will ever see each other again. You must promise me that you will send your wedding picture from America, so I will have proof that you are married."

"I will, Auntie, I promise."

We arrived at the Kherdian home in Kokinya in the late morning, and after we had had a light lunch, the men went outside, and with the help of several neighbors, they slaughtered and butchered a lamb.

The women went into the kitchen and began preparing the feast: pilaf, lavash, sarma, okra and beans, and pahklava.

By five o'clock the guests began arriving—neighbors, friends and relatives, as well as the musicians—and within an hour's time, the table was set and guests were seated. The evening began with hors d'oeuvres and toasts of *raki*, but before the first toast was made, Melkon's picture was passed around the table, so everyone could look at it and honor the fiancé.

The first toast was made by the teacher, who had been the family's spokesman:

"As guests of the fiancé's family, we are honored to participate in this joyous and holy occasion. And we are proud that the fiancée is a member of a prominent, highly respected family. And although they have been dispersed and decimated, as we all have been by the winds and fortunes of time, they have honored us this day with the presence of the fiancée's aunt, who lends great dignity to our table."

The guests gulped down their drinks—but I took only a sip of mine. Auntie had warned me that *raki* was strong, and she was right. I looked at her, and she made a sign with her eyes that I had better take it slowly.

The bridegroom's mother spoke next:

"We have searched hard to find a fitting bride for our son, and our search has not been in vain. Veron is a dignified young lady from a distinguished family, and we are honored to claim her for our Melkon. We can see with our own eyes that she will be a good wife, and we know our son will be a loving husband, because he has been a loving son. Although he is far from our hearth, he has never forgotten our plight, and he has been working single-mindedly to liberate us and deliver us safely to America. I give them my blessing!"

Her words made me happy. I remembered Auntie once saying to me that a mother's favorite son, once he has been blessed by her, is certain to have a good life.

I looked over at Auntie, and she was smiling. I was instantly warmed by her smile because I could see that she believed now that my decision had been a good one.

I thought Melkon's mother had finished, but she

was still standing, glass in hand. "May the very ground my son touches turn to gold," and emptying her glass, she sat down, with tears streaming down her wrinkled cheeks.

After a short silence, Aram, on whose right I was sitting, rose, and clearing his throat, began speaking:

"As the representative of my brother, I am honored to welcome all of you on this happy occasion. We hereby welcome Veron into our family, and we hope that we will bring her as much happiness as she has brought us by accepting the proposal of marriage of our eldest brother, Melkon. Our months of persistent effort have had a happy ending, and we know that our brother will be very happy with the woman who is to be his lifetime mate. We are pledged to deliver her safely to his door, and to see that their marriage is realized." Saying these last words, he looked down at me, and taking my hand, he motioned for me to rise. "In my brother's name I betroth thee with this ring," he said, and slipped Melkon's ring on my finger.

Veron Dumehjian married Melkon Kherdian in July 1924 in Waukegan, Illinois. They made their home in Racine, Wisconsin, and after seven years of marriage, a son, David, was born, followed by a daughter, Virginia. Veron Kherdian, now a widow, resides in Fresno, California.